Billy Graham
Evangelistic Association

DEAR FRIEND,

I am pleased to send you this copy of *Praying Through the Tough Times* by Dr. Lloyd John Ogilvie, who served as the honorary chairman of my father's 2004 Los Angeles Crusade.

When you are faced with circumstances beyond your control and you don't even know what to pray, the prayers in this book will guide you to see God's perspective. There are 100 prayers here, one for nearly any situation in life, including grief, pain, mistakes, trying relationships, and more. We pray that the Scripture verses and encouraging thoughts will help you find the peace you need.

The Billy Graham Evangelistic Association exists to take the message of Christ to all we can by every effective means available to us. Our desire is to introduce as many people as we can to the person of Jesus Christ, so that they might experience His love and forgiveness.

Your prayers are the most important way to support us in this ministry. We are grateful for the dedicated prayer support we receive. We are also grateful for those who support us with contributions.

If you would like to know more about the Billy Graham Evangelistic Association, please contact us:

In the U.S.:

> *Billy Graham Evangelistic Association*
> *1 Billy Graham Parkway*
> *Charlotte, North Carolina 28201-0001*
> *www.billygraham.org*
> *Toll-free: 1-877-2GRAHAM*
> *(1-877-247-2426)*

In Canada:

> *Billy Graham Evangelistic Association of Canada*
> *20 Hopewell Way NE*
> *Calgary, Alberta T3J 5H5*
> *www.billygraham.ca*
> *Toll-free: 1-888-393-0003*

We would appreciate knowing how this book or our ministry has touched your life. May God bless you.

Sincerely,

Franklin Graham
President

Praying Through THE Tough Times

Lloyd John OGILVIE

This **Billy Graham Library Selection** *special edition*
is published by the Billy Graham Evangelistic Association
with permission from Harvest House Publishers.

HARVEST HOUSE PUBLISHERS

EUGENE, OREGON

Cover by Koechel Peterson & Associates, Inc., Minneapolis, Minnesota

PRAYING THROUGH THE TOUGH TIMES

©2005 by Lloyd John Ogilvie
Published by the Billy Graham Evangelistic Association with permission from Harvest House Publishers.

A *Billy Graham Library Selection* designates materials that are appropriate to a well-rounded collection of quality Christian literature, including both classic and contemporary reading and reference materials.

ISBN 1-59328-035-1
Previous ISBN 0-7369-1430-7

Printed in the United States of America

CONTENTS

❧⟵❧

III. In Times of Pain

IV. In Times of Problems

V. In Times of Trying Relationships

VI. IN TIMES OF CONCERN OVER WORLD UNREST

VII. IN TIMES WHEN GOD HIMSELF IS THE ANSWER TO PRAYER

Acknowledgments

I want to express my deep gratitude to my assistant, Sandee Hastings, for her enthusiasm and affirmation of this book and for her excellent and tireless efforts in typing the manuscript for publication.

To Guy and Marion Martin
for their friendship through the years.
Tough times don't last;
faithful friends do!

God Himself Is the Answer

❦

TOUGH TIMES. WE ALL HAVE THEM. Perhaps you are in one of those times right now.

Tough times usually have something to do with loss:

- we are traumatized by the death of a loved one or close friend
- we are hurt when a profound disappointment comes our way
- we face the fracturing of a cherished relationship or endure conflict among people we love
- we see our hopes and dreams for our work put on hold
- we are under immense stress and strain
- we feel problems pile up
- we experience health problems, pain, or life-threatening illness

We've all lived in the tough times of panic over terrorism since 9/11. Soul-sized issues swirl around us, and we wonder if we can make any difference. And there are enough social problems in all our communities to keep us on edge.

It's often in tough times that we find it difficult to pray. When we need God most we find it hard to talk with Him. Our "why me's?" lead us into doubt, resentment, and finally a feeling of the absence of God. He hasn't left or changed, but we develop a low-grade agnosticism that leads to the neglect of prayer.

Then our "Lord, get me out of this!" eventually comes to "Lord, what do You want me to get out of this?" Our motto becomes "Things don't work out; God works out things!"

This book of prayers for tough times was written during my time of healing from grief after my wife of 52 years, Mary Jane, graduated to heaven. The prayers are in the first-person singular so they can be a very personal expression. They represent my own deepest thoughts and feelings, as well as those shared with me by fellow strugglers I've known and counseled through the many years of my ministry.

In all these prayers, I've tried to live in your skin and give wings to your own anguish or anxiety, or your praise and adoration.

I've put the prayers into categories of what I've found to be the most troublesome aspects of tough times. The "when I need" emphasis of most of the titles is for ready reference to what you may be going through right now. Also, it is my hope that this will be a book you will want to share with loved ones, friends, neighbors, and people at work when you want to help them receive comfort and courage in a tough time.

The undergirding conviction of these prayers is, *God Himself is the Answer.* What we all need in tough times is an intimate, healing, inspiring experience of His grace and goodness, peace and power.

Opposite each prayer are Scriptures, salient quotes from people who knew God's strength in tough times, and poems I've loved to remember and repeat when I needed a special boost and blessing. I hope they are as uplifting to you as they have been to me.

Prayer begins with God, and sweeps into our minds and hearts. He clarifies what He desires for us so that we can pray with boldness for what He is more ready to give than we may have been willing to ask. Prayer is the source of healing and hope in tough times.

My deepest longing is that this book will be a guide for honest, healing, and hopeful prayer for you whenever tough times come and the going is rough. God's promise to never leave or forsake us is absolutely true and reliable. I know!

—ᖗ *Lloyd John Ogilvie*

PART I

IN
TOUGH
TIMES

When I Need Faith
Today for Tomorrow

CHRIST, MY LORD, INDWELLING, INSPIRING, infusing power for courageous living in tough times, remind me that You only expect from me what You have placed or will place within me. You taught me to pray for daily bread. Thank You for the revelation that means bread today for tomorrow. You will give me today what I will need tomorrow. That's amazing, Lord!

I want to learn how to pray through tough times. Help me to know that You will equip me in advance as well as during the tough times. You will take up residence in me and provide the gift of faith to be applied to the crises I may have to confront. You are the Source of it all! You endow me with primary faith to accept You as Savior and Lord and invite You to make my soul Your home...but You also empower me with Your own faith to accomplish what will be the very best for my life. So I don't need to thrash about trying to conjure up enough faith to face tough times; rather, I can claim Your faith in me and what can be done by You for Your glory in me and around me.

As I pray through tough times You will release in me the aspect of Your character I most need for the circumstances ahead—courage, patience, endurance, discernment, wisdom, tenacity, and hope. I will be faithful because I will be full of Your faith to be expressed through me. You have offered me the abounding, unsearchable riches of Your own limitless resources. Today...for tomorrow! You are my strength in tough times. Amen.

Christ in you, the hope of glory.

COLOSSIANS 1:27

By grace you have been saved through faith,
and that not of yourselves;
it is the gift of God.

EPHESIANS 2:8

⧼⧽

F.B. Meyer shared the secret of enduring tough times:

It was first taught me by a grey-haired clergyman in the study of the Deanery at Southampton. Once when tempted to feel great irritation, he told us that he looked up and claimed the patience and gentleness of Christ and since then it had become the practice of his life to claim from Him the virtue of which he felt deficiency in himself. In hours of unrest, "Thy Peace, Lord." In hours of irritation, "Thy Patience, Lord." In hours of temptation, "Thy Purity, Lord." In hours of weakness, "Thy Strength, Lord." It was to me a message straight from the Lord. Till then I had been content to ridding myself of burdens; now I began to reach forth to positive blessings.*

There are two great words—claim God's fullness, and reckon that whatever you can claim is yours, although no answering emotion assures you that it is. Dare to act in faith, stepping out in the assurance that you have just what you have claimed, and doing just as you would do if you felt to have it.†

---

* F.B. Meyer, *Light on Life's Duties* (Chicago: Bible Institute Colportage Assoc., 1895), pp. 41-42.
† F.B. Meyer, *The Future Tenses of the Blessed Life* (Chicago: Fleming H. Revell, nd), pp. 120-121.

When I Need God's Faithfulness

Morning by morning new mercies I see.
All I have needed Thy hand hath provided;
*Great is Thy faithfulness, Lord, unto me!**

THOMAS O. CHISHOLM

ⲋⲋⲋⲋ

ALMIGHTY GOD, IT'S AN ASSURANCE of Your faithfulness I need in tough times. And all I need to do is turn to the Bible to hear the resounding affirmation of Your faithfulness. You told me Yourself, "My faithfulness shall be with you" (see Psalm 89:2,4). Jeremiah was comforted at a very difficult time and could say, "The Lord's mercies...are new every morning; great is Your faithfulness" (Lamentations 3:23). The psalmist couldn't express his gratitude enough: "I will sing of the mercies of the LORD forever; with my mouth will I make known Your faithfulness to all generations" (Psalm 89:1).

Even when I fail, I can repent and return to You. "If we confess our sins, He is faithful and just to forgive us our sins and to cleanse us from all unrighteousness" (1 John 1:9). How shall I respond to such grace? I will cast my burden on the Lord, and He will sustain me (see Psalm 55:22). And for all my worries? "Hear my prayer, O LORD, give ear to my supplications! In Your faithfulness answer me and in Your righteousness" (Psalm 143:1).

I need a character transplant from You as I face the challenges ahead today. Especially I want to be known for Your character trait of faithfulness. In spite of contradictory circumstances, I am committed to remain faithful to You, to my belief in Your goodness, and to the people who look to me for hope and inspiration for their own tough times. I pray that I may "be steadfast, immovable, always abounding in the work of the Lord," knowing that my labor "is not in vain in the Lord" (1 Corinthians 15:58). You are faithful! I can make it through today with that assurance. Amen.

---

* "Great Is Thy Faithfulness" by Thomas O. Chisholm, ©1923. Ren. 1951 Hope Publishing Co.

He Giveth More

He giveth more grace.
JAMES 4:6 KJV

He increaseth strength.
ISAIAH 40:29 KJV

Mercy unto you, and peace, and love, be multiplied.
JUDE 2 KJV

He giveth more grace when the burdens grow greater,
He sendeth more strength when the labors increase;
To added affliction He addeth His mercy,
To multiplied trials, His multiplied peace.

When we have exhausted our store of endurance,
When our strength has failed ere the day is half done,
When we reach the end of our hoarded resources,
Our Father's full giving is only begun.

His love has no limit, His grace has no measure,
His pow'r has no boundary known unto men;
For out of His infinite riches in Jesus,
He giveth, and giveth, and giveth again!

Annie Johnson Flint

When I Run Out of Zest

⁓⦵⦵⁓

ALMIGHTY GOD, SOVEREIGN OF ALL and personal Lord of my life, thank You for the gift of prayer. It is awesome that You who are Creator, Sustainer, and Redeemer of all, know me by name, and know my needs before I ask You. In this sacred moment I realize I need You more than anything You can give me. You created me to know and enjoy You as my Master and Friend. You who are so mighty are also magnanimous in my friendship with You. You love me, give me security, and replenish my hope. Time with You changes everything: My stress and strain are healed by Your peace, my worries are resolved by trusting You, my burdens are lifted off my back, my soul is replenished by Your indwelling Spirit. You care for me so much that You confront me when I am tempted with pride, anger, or impatience. You change my thinking when it gets muddled or confused. You have challenged me to pray for and care for others. You give me the courage to put the needs of Your kingdom first, above personal advantage.

I have every reason to be hopeful as I deal with the momentous and mundane issues this day will dish out. Give me the zest, verve, and vitality I need for today. Overcome my caution and concern. With vibrant expectation I will press on with enthusiasm. Amen.

Jesus said to them, "…If you have faith as a mustard seed, you will say to this mountain, 'Move from here to there,' and it will move; and nothing will be impossible for you."

MATTHEW 17:20

[He] is able to do exceedingly abundantly above all that we ask or think, according to the power that works in us.

EPHESIANS 3:20

He is able even to subdue all things to Himself.

PHILIPPIANS 3:21

He is able to aid those who are tempted.

HEBREWS 2:18

He is…able to save to the uttermost.

HEBREWS 7:25

[He] is able to keep you from stumbling.

JUDE 24

[He] is able to establish you.

ROMANS 16:25

He is able to keep what I have committed to Him.

2 TIMOTHY 1:12

Now commit your day to the Lord. He is able!

When I Need Hope

I know the thoughts that I think toward you, says the LORD, thoughts of peace and not of evil, to give you a future and a hope.

JEREMIAH 29:11

This I recall to my mind, therefore I have hope. Through the LORD's mercies we are not consumed, because His compassions fail not. They are new every morning; great is Your faithfulness.

LAMENTATIONS 3:21-23

DEAR GOD, I NEED HOPE! I long for authentic hope that is more than shallow optimism, wishful thinking, or anxious yearning.

You are the God of hope. It is awesome to be reminded that You have been thinking about me. Even better, it is profoundly comforting to know what You think about me and my circumstances. You want me to experience peace today and bright hope for tomorrow. You stay my mind on You. Your compassion for me stirs me; Your faithfulness never fails; Your timely interventions remind me that You keep Your gracious promises.

The sure foundation of my hope is Christ's resurrection from the dead, and the strength of my hope is in His presence and power. Today I intentionally commit all my concerns to You. This commitment is like a diminutive death to my tenacious tight grip of control. My sure hope now is for a resurrection to new life in my soul and miraculous resolution of those heart-aching worries. As You raised Jesus from the dead, You raise me out of the graves of discouragement. You fill me with a living hope that no trouble can destroy, no fear can disturb. I'm alive forever, and I'm going to live this day to the fullest.

Now focus my attention on people in my life who need hope. Make me a communicator of Your hope. Hope through me, God of hope!

Hope through me, God of Hope
Or never can I know
Deep wells of living streams of hope,
And pools of overflow.
O blessed Hope of God
Flow through me patiently,
Until I hope for everyone
As You have hoped for me.

—◦ *Amy Carmichael* ◦—

John Calvin, the impassioned Christian reformer, emphasized the crucial role of hope for kindling our faith. In his *Institutes of the Christian Religion*, he said that hope is the inseparable companion of faith.

> When this hope is taken away, however eloquently or elegantly we discourse concerning faith, we are convicted of having none. Hope is nothing else than the expectation of those things which faith has believed to have been truly promised by God…Hope nourishes and sustains faith…For no one except him who already believes His promises can look for anything from God, so again the weakness of our faith must be sustained and nourished by hope and expectation, lest it fail and grow faint…By unremitting renewing and restoring, it [hope] invigorates faith again and again with perseverance.

German theologian Jürgen Moltmann, in his benchmark work *The Theology of Hope*, puts it this way:

> In the Christian life faith has the priority, but hope the primacy. Without faith's knowledge of Christ, hope becomes a utopia and remains hanging in the air. But without hope, faith falls to pieces, becomes faint-hearted and ultimately a dead faith. It is through faith that a man finds the path of true life, but it is only hope that keeps him on that path. Thus it is that faith in Christ gives hope its assurance. Thus it is that hope gives faith in Christ its breadth and leads it into life.

When I Expect Too Little

⌘⌘⌘

BLESSED LORD JESUS, THANK YOU for the gifts of life, intellect, good memories, and daring dreams. I don't ask for challenges equal to my talent and training, education and experience; rather, I ask for opportunities equal to Your power and vision. Forgive me when I pare life down to what I could do on my own without Your power. Make me an adventuresome, undaunted person who seeks to know what You want done and attempts it because You will provide me with exactly what I will need to accomplish it. I thank You that tough times are nothing more than possibilities wrapped in negative attitudes. I commit the work of this day to You and will attempt great things for You because I know I will receive great strength from You.

May I live this day humbly on the knees of my heart, honestly admitting my human inadequacy and gratefully acknowledging Your power. Dwell in the secret places of my heart to give me inner security. Remind me of my accountability to You for all I say and do. Reveal Yourself to me. Be the unseen Friend beside me in every changing circumstance. Give me a fresh experience of Your palpable and powerful Spirit. Banish weariness and worry, discouragement and disillusionment. Often today may I hear Your voice, dear Christ, saying, "Come to me, all who are weary and heavy laden and I will give you rest." Lord, help me to rest in You and receive the incredible resiliency You provide. Thank You in advance for a truly productive day. In Your all-powerful Name, risen, reigning Christ. Amen.

LIMITED EXPECTATIONS

Filled with a strange new hope they came,
The blind, the leper, the sick, the lame.
Frail of body and spent of soul…
As many as touched Him were made whole.

On every tongue was the Healer's name,
Through all the country they spread His fame.
But doubt clung tight to his wooden crutch
Saying, "We must not expect too much."

Down through the ages a promise came,
Healing for sorrow and sin and shame,
Help for the helpless and sight for the blind,
Healing for body and soul and mind.

The Christ we follow is still the same,
With blessings that all who will may claim.
But how often we miss Love's healing touch
By thinking, "We must not expect too much."

—⌒ *Author unknown* ⌒—

When I Need 20/20 Hindsight

❦

GRACIOUS FATHER, HELP ME TO LIVE beyond the meager resources of my adequacies and learn that You are totally reliable when I trust You completely. You constantly lead me into challenges and opportunities that are beyond my strength and experience. I know that in every circumstance You provide me with exactly what I need.

Looking back over my life, I know I could not have made it without Your intervention and inspiration. And when I settle back on a comfortable plateau of satisfaction, suddenly You press me on to new levels of adventure. You are a disturber of false peace, the developer of dynamic character, and the ever-present deliverer when I attempt what I could not do on my own.

Sovereign of my life, I trust You, the ultimate Ruler. Give me acute hindsight so I can have 20/20 vision to see that You are at work in the shadowy realms of the often ambiguous turns of events. I grow in confidence as I remember that You have sustained me in crises at crucial times in my life. There is no panic in heaven; therefore, there can be peace in my soul in the midst of the human muddle of this uncertain time.

You have all power, You alone are almighty, and You are able to accomplish Your purposes and plans. You rule and overrule. When circumstances bring me results that are painful, give me patience to wait for a just resolution. Your intervening power is not limited: You are able to guide me about when and how to do what is best.

May this be a day in which I attempt something beyond my human adequacy and discover that You are able to provide the power to pull it off. Give me a fresh burst of excitement for the duties of this day so that I will be able to serve courageously. I will attempt great things for You and expect great things from You! Amen.

I have been a Christian for over 50 years. All through these years, the Lord has helped me face and conquer problems. In each difficulty I have learned more of Him and His ways. He's never let me down. And all I've discovered thus far is constantly drawn on when I confront present problems. We often talk about the "school of hard knocks." I'd rather call it the "school of gentle molding." The Lord shapes our character to be more like His own.

The eternal life, the life of faith, is simply a life of a higher vision. Faith is an attitude—a mirror set at right angle. To become like Christ is the only thing in the world worth caring for, the thing before which every ambition of man is folly, and all lower achievement vain.

 Henry Drummond

I remember the days of old;
I meditate on all Your works;
I muse on the work of Your hands.

Psalm 143:5

When I Need to Remember that What God Guides He Provides

❦

ALMIGHTY GOD, SOVEREIGN OF THIS PLANET within this universe among universes, by Your plan and power the Earth has revolved yet one more time, and You have blessed me with a new day. Today will be like no other day past or to come. I praise You for the privilege of being alive. Help me to trust You with all of the challenges and opportunities ahead of me today. I commit them to You. Go before me to prepare the way. I want to be so in tune with You that what I do and say will accomplish Your will.

May I sense Your presence and make this day one of constant inner conversation with You. As I practice Your presence, help me to trust You to guide my thinking. Give me a special measure of wisdom, insight, and discernment to tackle the problems that arise today. May this be a productive day as I hear and accept the psalmist's prescription for peace: "Cast your burden on the LORD, and He shall sustain you" (Psalm 55:22).

Belief in Your sovereignty gives me a sense of dependence that leads to true independence. All that I have and am is Your gift. When I am totally dependent on You for guidance and strength, I become completely free of fear and anxiety. What You guide, You provide. Trust in Your sovereignty provides supernatural power to accomplish what You give me to do for Your glory. And acceptance of Your sovereignty gives me courage. May Your sovereign authority abound in my life! Amen.

The Secret

I met God in the morning
When my day was at its best,
And His presence came like sunrise,
Like a glory in my breast.

All day long the Presence lingered,
All day long He stayed with me,
And we sailed in perfect calmness
O'er a very troubled sea.

Other ships were blown and battered,
Other ships were sore distressed,
But the winds that seemed to drive them
Brought to us a peace and rest.

Then I thought of other mornings,
With a keen remorse of mind,
When I too had loosed the moorings,
With the Presence left behind.

So I think I know the secret,
Learned from many a troubled way:
You must seek Him in the morning
If you want Him through the day!

—◦ *Ralph Spaulding Cushman* ◦—
from *Spiritual Hilltops*

When I Need to Forget Some Things and Never Forget Others

God has not given us a spirit of fear but of power and love and of a sound mind.

2 TIMOTHY 1:7

∞∞

DEAR GOD, TODAY GRANT ME what You promised: a spirit of power, a spirit of love, and the spirit of a sound mind. I need a sound mind in these tough days. A healed mind. Especially, I need for You to heal my memories and inspire my imagination.

Help me, dear God, to remember to forget some things and never to forget to remember others. I need to allow You to heal the hurting memories of the past: things I've done I should never have done, and things I've said I wish had never been spoken. Equally troubling are the things I wish I had not left unsaid or undone. In this time of honest prayer, I intentionally invite Your Spirit to dredge up memories You want to heal forever. I believe You can do it, Lord! Thank You for the magnificent gift of assurance of pardon.

Now, Lord, energize my imagination. Turpentine the layers of reserve and caution that immobilize my imagination. Clean it all away so I can picture what You want to do in and through me. Help me to see the new person You want me to be. In the same way, show me on the picture screen of my imagination what the people I love would be when filled with Your Spirit, what the situations that trouble me would be with Your solutions, and what the future could be if I let go of my icy grip and put it in Your hands. Thanks for healing me today! Amen.

I will give you a new heart and put a new spirit within you; I will take the heart of stone out of your flesh and give you a heart of flesh. I will put My Spirit within you and cause you to walk in My statutes, and you will keep My judgments and do them.

Ezekiel 36:26-27

Meditate within your heart on your bed, and be still. Offer the sacrifices of righteousness, and put your trust in the Lord.

Psalm 4:4-5

I meditate within my heart,
and my spirit makes diligent search.

Psalm 77:6

Delight yourself also in the Lord,
and He shall give you the desires of your heart.

Psalm 37:4

Having been justified by faith, we have peace with God through our Lord Jesus Christ, through whom also we have access by faith into this grace in which we stand, and rejoice in hope of the glory of God. And not only that, but we also glory in tribulations, knowing that tribulation produces perseverance; and perseverance, character; and character, hope. Now hope does not disappoint, because the love of God has been poured out in our hearts by the Holy Spirit who was given to us.

Romans 5:1-5

Open your heart to the Lord and trust Him with whatever causes you worry or anxiety today.

"He who believes in Me, as the Scripture has said, out of his heart will flow rivers of living water." But this He spoke concerning the Spirit, whom those believing in Him would receive; for the Holy Spirit was not yet given, because Jesus was not yet glorified.

John 7:38-39

When I Need to Check the Balance Sheet

❧❦❧

Gracious Father, source of all my blessings, I am amazed as I check the balance in my spiritual bank account. I begin this new day realizing that You have made an immense deposit of grace, strength, wisdom, and courage in my heart. And what's exciting is that You constantly will replenish my depleted resources throughout the future. Your love has no limits, Your spiritual resilience has no energy crisis, Your hope has no restrictions, and Your power has no ending.

Free me from the false assumption that I am adequate for life's challenges on my own. You promise to go before me. I will encounter no problem for which You have not prepared a solution; I will deal with no person whom You have not prepared to receive a blessing from You through me; I will face no challenge for which You will not make me capable for courageous leadership.

Lord, You know better than I what's ahead. Go before me to show the way. Then meet me in each person and situation. Anoint me with Your Holy Spirit that I may know what to say and do. Help me to anticipate and enjoy Your interventions. Here are my mind, will, and voice. Thank You for Your abiding presence and power. Give me the freedom and joy of knowing that Your special anointing will give me exactly what I need. Thank You for liberating me from the necessity of being adequate on my own. In the name of Christ, I accept Your deposit in my spiritual bank account. There never can be an overdraw! Amen.

By grace you have been saved through faith, and that not of yourselves; it is the gift of God, not of works, lest anyone should boast. For we are His workmanship, created in Christ Jesus for good works, which God prepared beforehand that we should walk in them.

Ephesians 2:8-9

You know the grace of our Lord Jesus Christ, that though He was rich, yet for your sakes He became poor, that you through His poverty might become rich.

2 Corinthians 8:9

God is able to make all grace abound toward you, that you, always having all sufficiency in all things, may have an abundance for every good work.

2 Corinthians 9:8

…that the God of our Lord Jesus Christ, the Father of glory, may give to you the Spirit of wisdom and revelation in the knowledge of Him, the eyes of your understanding being enlightened; that you may know what is the hope of His calling, what are the riches of the glory of His inheritance in the saints.

Ephesians 1:17-18

…the unsearchable riches of Christ.

Ephesians 3:8

All things are Yours…the world or life or death, or things present or things to come—all are Yours. And you are Christ's, and Christ is God's.

1 Corinthians 3:21-23

Jesus Christ opens wide the doors of the treasure-house of God's promises and bids us go and take what are ours.

— Corrie ten Boom —

When I Need to Choose to Be Chosen

❦

FAITHFUL FATHER, YOUR WORDS to Joshua so long ago sound in my soul as Your encouragement to me today. "I will not leave you nor forsake you. Be strong and of good courage" (Joshua 1:5-6). Thank You for the faithfulness and reliability of Your presence. Your love and guidance are not on-again, off-again. I can depend on Your steady flow of strength. Just to know that You are with me in all the ups and downs of life's demands is a great source of confidence. I can dare to be strong in the convictions You have honed in my heart and courageous in the application of them in my relationships and responsibilities.

Infuse my mind with a renewed sense of how much You have invested in me and how much You desire to do through me in the onward movement of Your kingdom. It is for Your name's sake, Your glory, and Your vision that You bless me. You guide and inspire me because You have great plans for me You want me to accomplish. You have chosen me; may I choose to be chosen today and live with spiritual self-esteem, motivated by this sense of chosenness. Your word for the day is, "Be not afraid, I am with you!" You are my Lord and Saviour. Amen.

You did not choose Me, but I chose you and appointed you
that you should go and bear fruit, and that your fruit
should remain, that whatever you ask the Father in My
name He may give you.

John 15:16

You are a chosen generation, a royal priesthood, a holy
nation, His own special people, that you may proclaim the
praises of Him who called you out of darkness into
His marvelous light.

1 Peter 2:9

I heard the voice of the Lord, saying, "Whom shall I send,
and who will go for Us?" Then I said, "Here am I! Send me."

Isaiah 6:8

As the elect of God, holy and beloved, put on tender
mercies, kindness, humility, meekness, longsuffering,
bearing with one another, and forgiving one another,
if anyone has a complaint against another;
even as Christ forgave you, so you also must do.
But above all these things put on love,
which is the bond of perfection.

Colossians 3:12-14

When I Need Peace of Mind

I am coming to the Lord,
Great petitions to Him I bring,
For His grace and mercy are such
That I never can ask too much!

∞⟲⟳∞

GRACIOUS GOD, I BELIEVE that in this time of prayer, my heart will wing its way to Your generous heart, and I will receive what I need from You, the very power that sways the universe. I pray not to get *Your* attention, but because You already have gotten *my* attention. I do not seek to convince You to listen to my petitions, because You have blessed and will bless me through my prayers. I know You desire to provide the unity and oneness of purpose with others I need. Long before I ask for Your wisdom and guidance, You have motivated the request in me. Thank You for Your grace, offered even before I ask and provided way beyond my deserving. Out of Your immense desire to bless me, imbue my mind with Your vision for what is best.

Blessed God, here I am at the beginning of another day. Help me to believe that what I commit to You this day will come to pass if You deem it best for me. I need to experience the peace of mind and body that comes when I do what You guide me to do and leave the results to You.

Bless me with the profound peace that comes from giving You my burdens and receiving Your resiliency and refreshment. May this be a great day because I, and all who live and work with me, decide to rest in Your presence and wait patiently for Your power to strengthen us. Through my Lord and Saviour. Amen.

Here is the secret of praying with power. Prayer starts with God. He is the initiator of the challenges of each lap of the race of life. And He never gives up on us regardless of our failures and weakness. With that assurance we can ask Nehemiah's question—"Can a person like me flee?" No! What the Lord did for Nehemiah through prayer, He will do for us and so much more.

We live on this side of Calvary. Christ endured the cross for our forgiveness. When He completed the atonement for us, He cried, "It is finished!" Because of that we never need to say in despair, "I'm finished!" We are never finished sharing the love and hope we have in Christ and working in His strength to accomplish each lap of the race. In a way, our confidence of eternal life enables us to run each lap with the assurance that we've already won the race!

When I Need to Trust More

Trust in the LORD with all your heart,
And lean not on your own understanding;
In all your ways acknowledge Him,
And He shall direct your paths.

PROVERBS 3:5-6

❦

GRACIOUS GOD, YOU ASK FROM ME only what You generously offer to give to me. You initiate this conversation called prayer because You want to bless me with exactly what I will need to live a faithful, confident, productive, joyous life today. You are for me—not against me.

Help me to live the hours of today knowing You are beside, are on my side, and offer me unlimited strength and courage besides. You will provide me insight and inspiration to confront and solve the problems I face. You will give me peace when my heart is distressed by the turbulence of our times. You will comfort me when I am afraid and need Your peace. You make me an overcomer when I feel overwhelmed. In response, I relinquish my imagined control over people and circumstances. I thank You for the power of faith I feel surging into my mind and heart. I trust in You, dear God, for You are my Lord and Saviour. Amen.

I will love You, O Lord, my strength.
The Lord is my rock and my fortress and my deliverer;
my God, my strength, in whom I will trust.

Psalm 18:1-2

In You, O Lord, I put my trust;
Let me never be ashamed;
Deliver me in Your righteousness.
Bow down Your ear to me,
Deliver me speedily;
Be my rock of refuge [strength],
A fortress of defense to save me.

Psalm 31:1-2

The Spirit Himself bears witness with our spirit that we are
children of God, and if children, then heirs—heirs of God
and joint heirs with Christ, if indeed we suffer with Him
that we may also be glorified together. For I consider
that the sufferings of this present time are not worthy
to be compared with the glory which shall be revealed in us.

Romans 8:16-18

...being confident of this very thing, that He who has
begun a good work in you will complete it until the day
of Jesus Christ.

Philippians 1:6

Rejoice always, pray without ceasing, in everything
give thanks; for this is the will of God in Christ Jesus
for you. Do not quench the Spirit.

1 Thessalonians 5:16-19

When I Need a Time of Attitude Adjustment

⊙≫⊶⊷≪⊙

GRACIOUS GOD, THE SOURCE OF INNER GRACE and outward joy, You have taught me that it is not just my aptitude, but my attitude, that determines the altitude of my success in Your work and in my relationships. I confess that often it is not You but the danger and difficulties of these days that dominate my inner feelings and control my attitudes. It's hard to be up for others when I get down on myself.

So thank You for this attitude adjustment time I call prayer, when I can admit any negative attitudes and submit to the transforming power of Your hope. You have been trying to teach me that true hope is faith in action and the constancy of faith in all contradictory circumstances. You've told me that there is no danger of developing eyestrain from looking at the bright side of things. There is a great need for this quality of hope in our nation. May the attitude of our people toward our present challenges be uplifted by their trust in You, the positive assurance of Your victory over the tyranny of terrorism, and the inspiring attitude of our leaders and all who work with them.

Now in the quiet of this time of honest prayer, I surrender my attitudes to Your transforming power. Give *me* a positive, inspiring attitude. The people around me have a right to see what trust in You can do to a person's attitudes. Make mine a reflection of Your hope and joy. Through Christ the attitude adjuster. Amen.

At the heart of the cyclone tearing the sky,
And flinging the clouds and flowers on,
Is a place of central calm;
And so in the roar of mortal things,
There's a place where my spirit sings,
In the hollow of God's palm.

 Edwin Markham
from *The Shoes of Happiness*

Our security is in God's hands:

See, I have inscribed you on the palms of My hands.
ISAIAH 49:16

"Into Your hand I commit my spirit."
PSALM 31:5

Your attitude should be the kind
that was shown to us by Jesus Christ.
PHILIPPIANS 2:5 TLB

…To be glad of life because it gives you the chance to
love and to work and to play and to look up at the
stars; to be satisfied with your possessions, but not
contented with yourself until you have made the best
of them; to despise nothing in the world except false-
hood and meanness, and to fear nothing except cow-
ardice; to be governed by your admirations rather
than your dislikes; to covet nothing that is your
neighbor's except his kindness of heart and gentleness
of manner; to think seldom of your enemies, often of
your friends, and every day of Christ.

Henry van Dyke

PRAYING THROUGH THE TOUGH TIMES

When I Am a Stingy Receiver

❧❧❧

GRACIOUS GOD, SOMETIMES I'm a stingy receiver who finds it difficult to open my tight-fisted grip on circumstances and receive the blessings that You have prepared. You know my needs before I ask You, but wait to bless me until I ask for Your help. I come to You now honestly to confess my needs. Lord, I need Your inspiration for my thinking, Your love for my emotions, Your guidance for my will, and Your strength for my body. I've learned that true peace and lasting serenity result from knowing that You have an abundant supply of resources to help me meet any trying situation, difficult person, or disturbing complexity, and so I say with the psalmist, "Blessed be the Lord, who daily loads us with benefits" (Psalm 68:19).

I gladly respond to the admonitions of the psalmist: "Commit your way to the LORD, trust also in Him, and He shall bring it to pass. Rest in the LORD, and wait patiently for Him" (Psalm 37:5,7). I prayerfully accept the vital verbs of this advice and apply them to my faith today: commit, trust, rest, wait. You have shown me that when I commit to You my life and my challenges, You go into action to bring about Your best for my life. Commitment opens the floodgates of my mind and my heart to the flow of Your power to help with people or problems that concern me. I trust in Your reliable interventions to free me from anxiety, and when I rest in Your everlasting arms, I experience spiritual resilience and refurbishment. All Your blessings are worth waiting for because nothing else gives me the strength and courage I really need. Thank You for Your faithful reliability. You, dear God, are my Lord and Saviour. Amen.

My God shall supply all your need according to
His riches in glory by Christ Jesus.

PHILIPPIANS 4:19

Beloved, I pray that you may prosper in all things
and be in health, just as your soul prospers.

3 JOHN 2

Teach me to do Your will,
For You are my God;
Your Spirit is good.
Lead me in the land of uprightness.

PSALM 143:10

Revive me, O LORD, for Your name's sake!
For Your righteousness' sake bring my soul out of trouble.

PSALM 143:11

All things that are exposed are made manifest by the light,
for whatever makes manifest is light. Therefore He says:
"Awake, you who sleep, arise from the dead, and
Christ will give you light." See then that you walk
circumspectly, not as fools but as wise, redeeming the time,
because the days are evil. Therefore do not be unwise,
but understand what the will of the Lord is.

EPHESIANS 5:13-17

I will keep on being filled with the Spirit.

EPHESIANS 5:18, AUTHOR'S TRANSLATION

When I Need to Be Thankful

❦

GRACIOUS GOD, I HAVE A GREAT NEED for the spiritual renewal that takes place when I return to an attitude of gratitude. In the midst of the problems I face at this time, I need the refreshing rejuvenation that comes when I turn from my trials and focus on thanksgiving for all my blessings. You have shown me that gratitude is not only the greatest of all the virtues, but the parent of all others. Any achievement without gratitude limps along the road of life; anything I accomplish without giving thanks becomes a source of pride. You desire my gratitude because You know it helps me grow; other people never tire of feeling the affirmation that is communicated when I express my thankfulness for them; and I require gratitude to avoid being self-serving and arrogant.

O God, I praise You for this nation of freedom and democracy. I repent of the pride of so many who entertain the idea that we are in charge of the destiny of this land. Grant me and them the true humility that comes from acknowledging that You are the Source of all we have and are. Now I am ready to thank You in advance for Your help in the resolution of the problems I face in these rough times. In the name of my Lord Jesus. Amen.

Thanksgiving

I will hope continually,
And will praise You yet more and more.
My mouth shall tell of Your righteousness
And Your salvation all the day,
For I do not know their limits.
I will go in the strength of the Lord GOD;
I will make mention of Your righteousness, of Yours only.

O God, You have taught me from my youth;
And to this day I declare Your wondrous works.
Now also when I am old and grayheaded,
O God, do not forsake me,
Until I declare Your strength to this generation,
Your power to everyone who is to come.

Also Your righteousness, O God, is very high,
You who have done great things;
O God, who is like You?
You, who have shown me great and severe troubles,
Shall revive me again,
And bring me up again from the depths of the earth.
You shall increase my greatness,
And comfort me on every side.

Also with the lute I will praise you—
And Your faithfulness, O my God!
To You I will sing with the harp,
O Holy One of Israel.
My lips shall greatly rejoice when I sing to You,
And my soul, which You have redeemed.

PSALM 71:14-23

❧❧❧

When I Feel Lonely

⁓⽊⊙⽊⁓

$\mathcal{L}$ORD, IT HAS BEEN AN ALARMING DISCOVERY. I can feel lonely in a crowd…when I have lots of friends and when I'm involved in a busy, seemingly productive life. You've helped me discover that loneliness is not the absence of people, but the absence of truly profound relationships in which I can talk out how I'm feeling, share my secrets, and be open about my hopes and dreams. It's also lonely when I don't share with vulnerability my big failures or little goofs.

At the same time, I feel lonely when there's no one with whom I can share my vision for the future, wild and impossible though it may seem at times. I guess a true friend is one with whom I can share the pain that makes me sad and the successes that make me glad. Loneliness seems to get worse when there's not someone who will cry with me and laugh with me, pick me up when life goes "bump," and bring me back down to reality when my plans soar with self-aggrandizement rather than self-sacrifice. I'm talking about true honesty that doesn't just condone, but gently confronts.

Now, Lord, here's the big discovery I'm making: I can't be to others the friend I need them to be to me until I have a truly satisfying relationship with You. Loneliness is the anxiety of unrelatedness. The first step out of it is to trust You as a close confidant. Then help me find people of Your choice to extend the circle, and I'll soon be ready to help heal the multitude of lonely people around me. It's awesome that You want a friend of the likes of me, but You do. You've told me that over and over again. Today, I'm going to believe You! Amen.

Loneliness, far from being a rare and curious phenomenon particular to myself and a few other solitary people, is the central and inevitable fact of human existence.

—‹ *Thomas Wolfe* ›—

He drew a circle that shut me out
Heretic, rebel, a thing to flout.
But love and I had the wit to win:
We drew a circle and took him in.

—‹ *Edwin Markham* ›—
from *The Shoes of Happiness*

Loneliness is none other than homesickness for God. Our loneliness is a "homing instinct." God has placed it within us. And intimate communion is our home. Christ is the way home to the Father.

I've found a friend; O such a Friend!
He loved me ere I knew Him;
He drew me with the cords of love,
And thus He bound me to Him.
And round my heart still closely twine
Those ties which naught can sever,
For I am His, and He is mine,
Forever and forever.

—‹ *James Grindlay Small* ›—

When I'm Worried

⋘∽⋙

GRACIOUS FATHER, IN WHOSE PRESENCE the dark night of the soul of worry is dispelled by the dawn of Your love, I thank You for helping me overcome my worries. You have taught me that worry is like interest paid on difficulties before it comes due. It's rust on the blade that dulls my capacity to cut through trouble and lance the infection of anxiety. Your Word is true: Worry never changes anything but the worrier, and that change is never positive. Worry is impotent to change tomorrow or redo the past. All it does is sap my strength.

I confess that I fear I may have to face alone the problems and perplexities that come to me. My worry is really loneliness for You, dear God. In this moment of prayer I surrender all my worries to You and thank You for Your triumphant promise: "Do not be afraid—I will help you. I have called you by name—you are Mine. When you pass through the deep waters, I will be with you; your troubles will not overwhelm you" (Isaiah 43:1-2, author's translation).

In this intimate moment with You, I invite You to help me overcome my worry habit. Grant me fresh strength. I admit my needs and accept Your power. Through Christ who has defeated the destructive power of worry once and for all. Amen.

Do not worry about your life, what you will eat or what you
will drink; nor about your body, what you will put on.
Is not life more than food and the body more
than clothing?…For your Heavenly Father knows that
you need all these things. But seek first the kingdom of
God and His righteousness, and all these things shall be
added to you. Therefore do not worry about tomorrow,
for tomorrow will worry about its own things.
Sufficient for the day is its own trouble.

MATTHEW 6:25,32-34

Out of the depths I have cried to You, O LORD; Lord,
hear my voice! Let Your ears be attentive to the voice of my
supplications. If You, LORD, should mark iniquities,
O Lord, who could stand? But there is forgiveness with You,
that You may be feared.

PSALM 130:1-4

I have loved you with an everlasting love;
therefore with lovingkindness I have drawn you.

JEREMIAH 31:3

It is good to give thanks to the LORD, and to sing praises to
Your name, O Most High; to declare Your lovingkindness
in the morning, and Your faithfulness every night.

PSALM 92:1-2

The LORD your God in your midst, the Mighty One, will
save; He will rejoice over you with gladness, He will quiet
you with His love, He will rejoice over you with singing.

ZEPHANIAH 3:17

Show me Your ways, O LORD; teach me Your paths.
Lead me in Your truth and teach me, for You are the God
of my salvation; on You I wait all the day.

PSALM 25:4-5

PRAYING THROUGH THE TOUGH TIMES

When I Need Meaning in My Work

❧❧❧

GRACIOUS FATHER, WHO HAS GIVEN ME LIFE, bless me today in the work I will do. I praise You for work that can be done as an expression of my worship of You. I bring the meaning of my faith to my work rather than trying to make my work the ultimate meaning of my life. With that perspective, I seek to do everything to Your glory. I pray for mental alertness, emotional stability, and physical strength to achieve excellence in all I do. Thank you for Your companionship in tasks great and small. It is awesome to contemplate that You who are in control of the universe have placed me in charge of what You want to accomplish through me.

Fill me with Your grace and make me a cheerful person who makes others happier because I am with them. Make me a blessing and not a burden, a lift and not a load, a delight and not a drag. It's great to be alive! Help me make a difference because of the difference You have made in me.

Sometimes my long days of work and my nights of too little rest run together. I need You. I praise You for Your love that embraces me and gives me security, Your joy that uplifts me and gives me resiliency, Your peace that floods my heart and gives me serenity, and the presence of Your Spirit that fills me and gives me strength and endurance.

I dedicate this day to You. Help me to realize that it is by Your permission that I breathe my next breath, and by Your grace that I am privileged to use all the gifts of intellect and judgment that You provide. Give me a perfect blend of humility and hope, so that I will know You have given me all that I have and am and have chosen to bless me this day. My choice is to respond and to commit myself to You.

I thank You for the attitude change that takes place when I remember I am called to glorify You in my work and to work with excellence to please You. Help me to realize how privileged I am to be able to work, earn wages, and provide for my needs. Thank You for the dignity of work. Whatever I do, in word or deed, I do it to praise You. Amen.

Whatever you do in word or deed, do all in the name of the
Lord Jesus, giving thanks to God the Father through Him.

COLOSSIANS 3:17

Whatever you do, do all to the glory of God.

1 CORINTHIANS 10:31

Most of us will work 160,000 hours during our lifetime. If
we take few vacations and work after hours, many of us will
work about 200,000 hours. A housewife will work more than
290,000. Work can be either a drudgery or a delight. We
either bring meaning to our work or make work the meaning
of our lives.

> I simply argue that the cross be raised again in the
> center of the marketplace as well as on the steeple of
> churches. I want to recover the truth that Jesus was
> not crucified on an altar between two candlesticks,
> but on a garbage heap at a crossroads of the world, a
> cosmopolitan crossroads where they had to describe
> who He was in Latin, in Greek and in Hebrew, where
> soldiers gambled and cynics talked smut.

— George McCloud —

Christ died in a real world then and occupies a real place in
our lives now. He must be at the center of the real issues of life.
The central questions are, "How can I work more effectively
for Christ on the job? Do I enjoy Him at work?"

When I Feel Depleted

❧❧❧

ALMIGHTY GOD, WHEN I HUMBLE MYSELF and confess my aching need for You, You lift me up and grant me opportunities beyond my imagination. When I try to make it on my own, claiming recognition for myself, eventually I become proud and self-sufficiently arrogant. Keeping up a front of adequacy becomes demanding. Pride blocks my relationship with You and debilitates deep, supportive relationships with others.

Father, help me accept my humanity. I need You, and life is a struggle when I pretend I have it all together. I come to You with honest confession of the times I forgot You—went for hours, even days, without asking for Your help, and endured life's pressures as if I could be my own source of strength.

I invite You to fill my depleted resources with Your Spirit. I want to let You love me, forgive me, renew me, and grant me fresh joy. To this end I admit my needs and accept Your power.

Thank You for the problems that make me more dependent on You for guidance and strength. When I have turned to You in the past, You have given me strength and skills I needed. Thank You, Lord, for taking me as I am with all my human weaknesses, and using me for Your glory. May I always be known for the immensity of my gratitude—my thankfulness for the way that You pour out Your wisdom and vision when I humbly cry out to You for help. I am profoundly grateful. In Christ, my dear Saviour's name.

"God resists the proud, but gives grace to the humble"...Humble yourselves in the sight of the Lord, and He will lift you up.

JAMES 4:6,10

Humble yourselves under the mighty hand of God, that He may exalt you in due time, casting all your care upon Him, for He cares for you.

1 PETER 5:6-7

If evil at its overwhelming worst has already been met and mastered, as in Jesus Christ it has; if God has got His hands on this baffling mystery of suffering in its direct, most defiant form, and turned its most awful triumph into uttermost, irrevocable defeat; if that in fact has happened, and on that scale, are you to say it cannot happen on the infinitely lesser scale of our own union with Christ through faith? In heart-breaking things that happen to us, those mental agonies, those spiritual midnights of the soul, we are "more than conquerors," not through our own valor or stoic resolution, not through a creed or code or philosophy, but "through Him who loved us"—through the thrust and pressure of the invading grace of Christ.

—⁓ *James S. Stewart* ⁓—

When My Agenda Is Packed

$\mathcal{A}$LMIGHTY GOD, SOURCE OF STRENGTH for tired bodies, stressed-out emotions, and strained minds, I pray for the courage to press on. Infuse me with profound trust that will give me the second wind of Your divine energy, resiliency, and endurance. Remind me that You called me to serve You, promised Your hour-by-hour replenishment, and assured me You would be with me in demanding times. May I turn to You constantly throughout this day. As I draw on Your wisdom, give me insight and discernment; as I depend on Your Spirit, grant me patience; as I receive Your peace, set me free of anxiety and tension; and as I invite You to guide me, show me workable solutions and creative compromises. And now as I run another lap of life's relay race, help me to cheer others, rather than tripping them up.

Your love and mercy continue, fresh as the new morning, as sure as the sunrise. You are my strength, and again I put my hope in You.

Lord, a packed agenda awaits me today. May my mind be power-packed with Your wisdom. Grant me physical stamina for the strain of a busy schedule, the demands of decisions, the sapping strain of conflict, and the personal problems I often think I must carry alone. Help me to claim Your promise, "As your days, so shall your strength be." Pour Your Spirit into the well of my soul and give me supernatural resiliency and resourcefulness. I accept this day as Your gift, enter into its challenges with eagerness and into its possibilities with a positive attitude. As I grow in Your joy, help me to remind my face to radiate it. Through Christ, who gives me more strength as the challenges grow greater. Amen.

Think of the crucial times the offer to take courage is made in the New Testament. It was spoken to the paralytic in Matthew 9:2 when the Lord said, "Take courage…your sins are forgiven" (NASB). The same assurance was spoken to the woman who pressed through the crowd and touched the Master. "Take courage; your faith has made you well" (Matthew 9:22 NASB). The people around blind Bartimaeus said it when Jesus responded to his plea. "Take courage…He is calling you" (Mark 10:49 NASB). And the disciples in the Upper Room heard these gracious words, "In the world you have tribulation, but take courage; I have overcome the world" (John 16:33 NASB).

In prayer the Lord takes hold of us with one hand and offers courage with the other. Horatius Bonar experienced this and penned a triumphant assurance:

Thy love to me, O God,
Not mine, O Lord, to Thee,
Can rid me of this dark unrest and set my spirit free.
Let me no more my comfort draw
From my frail hold on Thee.
Rather in this rejoice with awe
Thy mighty grasp on me.

We can take it only because the Lord has taken us. He has a tight grip on us.

Courage is fear which has said its prayers. If we are not attempting something which creates the human reaction of fear we are probably not living life as it was meant to be lived. Fear in the soul-stretching challenges of these days drives us to prayer. Eddie Rickenbacker knew what he was talking about when he said that courage is doing what you're afraid to do. There is no courage unless you're scared and are driven to your knees. Thomas Fuller, English divine and author (1608–1661), said, "Fear can keep a man out of danger, but courage can support him in it."

Winston Churchill said, "Courage is the greatest virtue because it makes possible all the rest. Never give up. Never give up! Never, never give up!"

When I Feel Soul'd Out

❧❧❧

GRACIOUS LORD, INSIDE ME IS that sacred sanctuary of the soul, the port of entry for Your Spirit, the place You live in me, and the portion of me that determines the development of my character and the direction for my life. I join with the psalmist's longing for You to heal my soul with Your forgiveness, uplift my soul with Your inspiration, quiet my soul with Your peace, sustain my soul with Your patience, and calm my soul with Your pacing and timing. May the soul of the matter for me today be to express what You have placed in my soul.

In the ongoing schedule of my life, I tend to lose one of the most precious gifts You offer me: a sense of expectancy. As I live in this new day, help me to expect great things from You and to attempt great things for You. I will perform the same old duties differently because You will have made me a different person, filled with Your love, joy, peace, and patience. I commit to You the challenges and opportunities ahead, expecting Your surprises—serendipities of Your interventions—to work things out. Give me freedom to cooperate with You. Inspire in me a positive attitude towards life because I know You will maximize my efforts, assist me when dealing with difficult people, and help me care for those in need. Bring on life, Lord; filled with Your Spirit, I am expecting wonderful things to happen!

So I say with the psalmist, "Bless the LORD, O my soul; and all that is within me, bless His holy name! Bless the LORD, O my soul, and forget not all His benefits" (Psalm 103:1-2). Lord God of hosts, be with me yet, lest I forget! Amen.

He restores my soul.

PSALM 23:3

Come and hear, all of you who fear God, and I will declare
what He has done for my soul. I cried to Him with my
mouth, and He was extolled with my tongue. If I regard
iniquity in my heart, the LORD will not hear. But certainly
God has heard me; He has attended to the voice of my
prayer. Blessed be God, who has not turned away
my prayer, nor His mercy from me!

PSALM 66:16-20

Fear not, I will help you.

ISAIAH 41:13

Our help is in the name of the LORD,
who made heaven and earth.

PSALM 124:8

We must prayerfully cultivate this sacred confidence
in the possibilities of the unlikely. We can never be
successful helpers of the Lord unless we can see the
diamond in the soot, and the radiant saint in the dis-
regarded publican. It is a most gracious art to cultivate, this of discerning a man's possible excellencies
even in the blackness of his present shame. To see the
future best in the present worst, that is the true per-
ception of a child of light.*

---

* John Henry Jowett, *My Daily Meditation* (New York: Fleming H. Revell Company, 1914), p. 196.

When I Need to Let Go

⁜

OMNIPRESENT LORD GOD, there is no place I can go where You have not been there waiting for me; there is no relationship in which You have not been seeking to bless the people with whom I am involved; there is no task You have given me to do for which You are not present to help me accomplish. I need not ask to come into Your presence; Your presence with me creates the desire to pray. You delight in guiding me to pray for what You are more ready to give than I may be prepared to ask.

You are here. I do not need to convince You to bless my life. You have shown me how much You love and care. You want the very best for me and have chosen me, through whom You want to work to accomplish Your plans. Help me to see myself as Your agent. Bless me with Your power. Keep me fit physically, secure emotionally, and alert spiritually. So much depends on my trust in You and pursuit of Your guidance. May awe and wonder capture me as I realize all You have put at my disposal to ensure that I succeed. Thank You for the biblical assurance "that all things work together for good to those who love God, to those who are the called according to His purpose" (Romans 8:28). You are my Lord and Saviour. Amen.

GOD HERE, THERE, EVERYWHERE

May the wisdom of God instruct me,
The eye of God watch over me,
The ear of God hear me,
The word of God give me sweet talk,
The hand of God defend me,
The way of God guide me.
Christ be with me.
Christ before me.
Christ in me.
Christ under me.
Christ over me.
Christ on my right hand.
Christ on my left hand.
Christ on this side.
Christ on that side.
Christ in the head of everyone to whom I speak.
Christ in the mouth of every person who speaks to me.
Christ in the eye of every person who looks upon me.
Christ in the ear of everyone who hears me today.
Amen.

—⁖ *Saint Patrick* ⁖—

PART II

IN TIMES
OF GRIEF

When I Endure Grief

❧❧❧

LORD OF ALL LIFE, I COME TO YOU for the healing of the griefs of life. I feel grief whenever I stand in the midst of shattered dreams. For me, it's essentially my response to having to say "goodbye" with finality: goodbye at death's door; goodbye at the collapse of something I've worked for; goodbye to the past and the what-might-have-beens of life. Grief comes after the intense emotional shock of final separation from a loved one, a relationship, a place, or a comfortable surrounding. I experience similar thoughts and emotions of grief when a loved one dies, during and after the memorial service, when I've failed, when a relationship is broken, or when a program in which I might have invested my ego and future security is lost.

Is there such a thing as "good grief"? Over the years You have taught me that something is good if it fulfills its purpose. What causes my grief I'm reluctant to call "good" unless it achieves its intended purpose of healing my disturbed mind and distressed emotions.

Lord, help me to accept that grief is the healing process given me as Your gift. I feel pain, and it is good to know that the process is taking place. When a loved one dies I experience excruciating reactions. I tremble, shiver, and feel depleted. I ache emotionally. I'm tempted to have outbursts, or withdraw, deny, or become angry. Most of all I need to find some vent to my anguish. I need to talk to You. Until I know what to say, tears flow. In it all I'm coming to grips with the reality of my loss. And what's truly amazing is that You are there listening and offering Your healing of my grief. Thank You, Lord! Amen.

Most assuredly I say to you that you will weep and
lament...you will be sorrowful, but your sorrow will be
turned into joy.

JOHN 16:20

There would be no grief if we did not care. Loss is real and
we feel the pain. But good grief is absolutely necessary if we are
to live again after a heart-racking loss of someone dear to us.

For this slight momentary affliction is preparing for us
an eternal weight of glory beyond all comparison, because
we look not to the things that are seen...for the things
that are seen are transient, but the things that are
unseen are eternal.

2 CORINTHIANS 4:17-18 RSV

God will wipe away every tear from their eyes;
there shall be no more death, nor sorrow, nor crying.
There shall be no more pain,
for the former things have passed away.

REVELATION 21:4

Nothing can make up for the absence of someone
whom we love. It is nonsense to say that God fills the
gap; He doesn't fill it, but on the contrary, He keeps
it empty and so helps us to keep alive our former
communion with each other, even at the cost of pain.
The dearer and richer our memories, the more difficult the separation. But gratitude changes the pangs
of memory into a tranquil joy. The beauties of the
past are borne, not as a thorn in the flesh, but as a
precious gift in themselves.

—*Dietrich Bonhoeffer*

PRAYING THROUGH THE TOUGH TIMES

When Grief Is Not an Enemy

❧❧❧

DEAR GOD, YOU ARE HELPING ME LEARN that grief is no more an enemy than is sleep, rest, or the physical healing process of the body. It is Your gift of the cleansing and healing of my emotions. Grief is itself a medicine.

Now I want to thank You for affirming that my grief is an evidence of my capacity to love. Lack of authentic grief is a sign of shallow love and an inability to care deeply. I hear You, Lord! There would be no grief if I did not care. Loss is real, and I feel the pain. It's not a sign of weakness, but of strength.

It's not easy to befriend grief and go through it creatively. Remind me that there is no such thing as unexpressed grief. I know that when it is repressed it only comes out in another form. I need to let my grief flow. With You I can let it out and tell You how I'm really feeling. When I do, I begin to think more clearly about the benefits of eternal life and the dawn of a new day for the one I've lost. This life is but a fraction of eternity; death is not an ending but a transition in living for those who know You through Christ, the cross, and an empty tomb.

And yet, You help me go through the emotional as well as the thinking process. It is a supreme gift from You to be able to let go and accept my loss. You don't offer shabby shibboleths or trite phrases. You are right here with me: loving, comforting, holding me while I sob. Only after that can I greet the future as a friend. Thank You, eternal healer of grief. Amen.

The joy of the LORD is your strength.

NEHEMIAH 8:10

You now have sorrow; but I will
see you again and your heart will rejoice,
and your joy no one will take from you.

JOHN 16:22

You have made known to me the ways of life;
You will make me full of joy in Your presence.

ACTS 2:28

Blessed are you who weep now, for you shall laugh.

LUKE 6:21

There is no circumstance, no trouble, no testing, that
can ever touch me until, first of all, it has gone past
God and past Christ, right through to me. If it has
come that far, it has come with a great purpose,
which I may not understand at the moment. But I
refuse to become panicky, as I lift up my eyes to him
and accept it as coming from the throne of God for
some great purpose of blessing to my own heart.

— *Alan Redpath* —

I came from God, and I'm going back to God, and I
won't have any gaps of death in the middle of my life.

— *George MacDonald* —

When Grief Is Wasted

⌾⌾⌾

*L*ORD, HELP ME NOT TO WASTE my grief. It is time for growth and for new maturity. Don't let me get caught in the quicksand of "if onlys." If there is something I could or should have done, help me confess that to You and experience Your healing.

Remind me that self-pity is a waste of good grief. "What did I do to deserve this?" or "Why is life treating me so badly?" are irrelevant questions. It's arrogant to barrage You with the silly question, "Why did this happen to me after all the good I've done and the responsible life I've tried to live?" Resentment is equally unproductive. You have been encouraging me to learn that grief can be one of the most creative times in my life. I ponder the words of Amy Carmichael: "The eternal essence of a thing is not in the thing itself but in one's reaction to it. The distressing situation will pass, but one's reaction toward it will leave a moral and spiritual deposit in our character which is eternal."

In the healing of my grief, help me not to make You the enemy. You did not cause my loss, but You are here to help me endure it. Forgive me if I ever blame You and miss Your blessing. I live in a world of germs, illness, and trauma. You don't send trouble; there's already enough to go around. But You have settled the most important issues of life on Calvary, in an Open Tomb, and in an Upper Room at Pentecost. Once again, I accept Your love, and invite Your Spirit to live in me to heal my grief—and I claim that neither death nor anything else can ever separate me from You, now and forever! Amen.

No sorrow touches man until it has been filtered through the heart of God.

— Joseph D. Blinco —

What God Hath Promised

God hath not promised skies always blue,
Flower-strewn pathways all our lives through;
God hath not promised sun without rain,
Joy without sorrow, peace without pain.

God hath not promised we shall not know
Toil and temptation, trouble and woe;
He hath not told us we shall not bear
Many a burden, many a care.

God hath not promised smooth roads and wide,
Swift, easy travel, needing no guide;
Never a mountain rocky and steep,
Never a river turbid and deep.

But God hath promised strength for the day,
Rest for the labor, light for the way,
Grace for the trials, help from above,
Unfailing sympathy, undying love.

— Annie Johnson Flint —

When I Need to Let God Heal My Grief

❦❦❦

Dear God, the Healing Power of the world, thank You for helping me realize You don't just send healing of grief. You *are* healing. The healing process of creative grief takes place when I allow You to love me profoundly.

Sometimes this is not easy. When I need You the most I'm tempted to cry out accusingly, "How could You allow this to happen?" When I am honest with You about my feelings, I'm able to think clearly about Your own grief over Your fallen creation and the rebellion of humankind.

The most awesome choice You ever made was to give humankind freedom of will and choice. You didn't create me as a marionette; I was created to know You, love You, and obey You. I know the sad tale of what humankind did with this freedom, from Adam onward. I live in a world fractured off from Your original purpose. It is a world filled with suffering. Tragedies occur.

Remind me again: You do not send suffering. You grieve because You love me. In Christ You entered into my human grief. Your Son knew the anguish of rejection, hostility, denial, and betrayal, and the suffering of death for the sins of the world.

In times of grief I return to the cross. I cling to the assurance of Your love and forgiveness. Grief alone does not heal me. It is creative only as I receive Your love. Feelings follow thought. I stand on the rock of Christ who lived, died, rose again, and is with me now. Heaven has begun for me. I am alive forever and can face the temporary griefs of life. Amen.

He heals the brokenhearted, binding up their wounds.

PSALM 147:3 TLB

May the God of peace who brought up our Lord Jesus from
the dead, that great Shepherd of the sheep, through the
blood of the everlasting covenant, make you complete in
every good work to do His will, working in you what is well
pleasing in His sight, through Jesus Christ, to whom be
glory forever and ever. Amen.

HEBREWS 13:20-21

We do not lose heart. Even though our outward man
is perishing, yet the inward man is being renewed
day by day. For our light affliction, which is but for
a moment, is working for us a far more exceeding
and eternal weight of glory, while we do not look at
the things which are seen, but at the things which are not
seen. For the things which are seen are temporary,
but the things which are not seen are eternal.

2 CORINTHIANS 4:16-18

When this corruptible has put on incorruption, and this
mortal has put on immortality, then shall be brought to pass
the saying that is written: "Death is swallowed up in victory.
O Death, where is your sting? O Hades, where
is your victory?"

1 CORINTHIANS 15:54-55

When I Need to See
the Morning Star

❦

DEAR CHRIST, YOU NEVER PROMISED I would not endure things that cause grief, but You did offer that I would have peace. You are the "Bright and Morning Star" (Revelation 22:16). Just as the evening star signals the end of the day, the morning star promises the end of the night and the coming of a new day. It is the star that appears and shines most brilliantly just before dawn.

Christ, You are that to me in my grief. In the dark night of mental and emotional turmoil over the varied things that bring me into the process of grief, You come with a promise of a new beginning. I can endure the dark, murky night of grief with Your encouragement. Your presence right now as the Morning Star gives me the assurance that there will be an end of the night. You rise, not in the firmament of the sky, but in my heart. Peter encouraged the early Christians to endure suffering "until the day dawns and the morning star rises in your hearts" (2 Peter 1:19).

Saviour, You have been very honest with me that the peace I need so desperately would be experienced in the perplexities of life: "These things I have spoken to you, that in Me you may have peace. In the world you will have tribulation; but be of good cheer, I have overcome the world" (John 16:33).

Indeed You have! You are victor over death, triumphant over the evil schemes of Satan. I ask for Your peace to overcome my sadness, Your joy to pulsate in my emotions, and Your hope to lift me out of the doldrums.

The mists of dawn are lifting, the Morning Star shines brightly, and a new day is beginning! Amen.

The Morning Star Pierces the Darkness

The apostle John was alone on the Island of Patmos, a political prisoner of Rome. He was in a cave looking out onto the Aegean Sea. The Lord Jesus appeared to the grief-stricken apostle. He was filled with deep grief for the churches of Asia Minor and what seemed to be happening to the cause of Christ in the world. To him the reigning Christ revealed His supremacy over life and death, frustration and pain, loss and loneliness. He gave John the secret for enduring grief in the interim between what he was facing and Christ's final victory.

Into the dark night of John's heart came a shaft of light. He looked into the sky and saw the morning star rising. A shaft of light pierced his soul as Christ said to him, "I am the Root and Offspring of David, the Bright and Morning star" (Revelation 22:16). It was what John needed. And so do we.

That gives us background for the grief-healing assurance of the prayer you just prayed with me with first-person particularity. Together you and I have experienced what Christ also said to the troubled, pressured, persecuted church at Thyatira: "Hold fast what you have, until I come. He who conquers and who keeps my works until I come, I will give him power...And I will give him the morning star." There's our motto for grief: "Hold fast! The Morning Star is rising in the black, otherwise starless night of our grief!"

When I Need Courage
to Say "Goodbye"

❦

Dear Lord, thank You for what You are teaching me about grief. You keep bringing me back to the necessity of eventually saying "goodbye" to a loved one who has graduated to heaven. When I have owned and befriended my grief, have felt through my very human reactions, and have grown in deeper trust in You, there does come a time of release. I think of the Scots expression, " 'Bye for just now. See you in the morning!"

Parting is sweet sorrow only when the sweetness is based on the confidence that we will see a loved one again in heaven. For now, however, you keep reminding me that the physical presence of a loved one is no longer with me. Thank you for cherished memories and for that mystical bond between the living and the graduated in heaven, but free me to live again, making the most of each day until my own graduation.

Thank You for Your ordained duration of mourning. You do signal me when it is the end of the night. You have all power in heaven and earth to heal me and give me a new beginning when I have the courage to say goodbye to what has been and can never be again. You make me ready to experience what I never dared dream would be possible for the future.

Lord Jesus, You promised, "Blessed are those who mourn, for they shall be comforted" (Matthew 5:4). I have mourned and am open to be comforted by You. Your comfort neutralizes the toxins of bitterness and cynicism. Thank You for making me whole!

＊＊＊

I will turn their mourning into gladness;
I will give them comfort and joy instead of sorrow.

JEREMIAH 31:13 NIV

There is a time for everything, and a season for every activity
under heaven…A time to weep and a time to laugh,
a time to mourn and a time to dance.

ECCLESIASTES 3:1,4 NIV

＊＊＊

God washes the eyes by tears until they can behold
the invisible land where tears shall come no more.

—◦ *Henry Ward Beecher* ◦—

Not until each loom is silent
And the shuttles cease to fly
Will God unroll the pattern
And explain the reason why.
The dark threads are as useful
In the Weaver's skillful hand
As the threads of gold and silver
For the pattern He has planned.

—◦ *Anonymous* ◦—

The LORD will be your everlasting light,
and your days of sorrow will end.

ISAIAH 60:20 NIV

When I Suffer with Christ

Lord Jesus, You told me to abide in You and that You would abide in me. Your indwelling presence turns grim grief into good grief. From within, You assure me I am loved and You give me the power to endure. Thank You for liberating me from within. My relentless questioning—"why, why?"—is replaced by the power to trust that what You have allowed life to give or withhold can be used for my growth in what's ultimately important—my relationship with You. Whatever is my loss, it is more than balanced by the assurance that I'm never called to go through anything that You will not provide strength and courage to conquer.

With awe and wonder I contemplate Paul's bracing truth, "The Spirit Himself bears witness with our spirit that we are children of God, and if children, then heirs—heirs of God and joint heirs with Christ, if indeed [since] we suffer with Him, that we may also be glorified together" (Romans 8:16-17). Suffering with You, Christ, puts grief into perspective. You are with me and in me. There will be suffering, but You will help me through it. What happens to me can be used for Your glory and for the glory of being made more completely in Your image. When I surrender my grief to You, I finally feel the pain let up, and I suddenly feel a new enthusiasm for the future. At last, I know freedom. "Now the Lord is the Spirit; and where the Spirit of the Lord is, there is liberty. But we all, with unveiled face, beholding as in a mirror the glory of the Lord, are being transformed into the same image from glory to glory, just as by the Spirit of the Lord" (2 Corinthians 3:17-18).

I pause to reflect on all that is mine because I am a joint-heir with You. I belong to the Father's forever family; I am loved and forgiven; I have come alive to life as it was meant to be lived now, and I will live forever; heaven has begun, and fear of death no longer has power over me; I am being transformed into Christ's image; and I have power to confront the problems and perplexities of life. I praise You, Lord!

When in affliction's valley
I'm treading the road of care
My Savior helps me carry
My cross so heavy to bear
Though all around me is darkness
Earthly joys all flown;
My Saviour whispers His promise
Never to leave me alone.

—o *Ludie D. Pickett* o—

I cannot do without Thee
I cannot stand alone
I have no strength or goodness
Nor wisdom of my own
But Thou, beloved Savior
Art all in all to me
And perfect strength in weakness
Is mine when I lean on Thee.

—o *Anonymous* o—

My grace is sufficient for you, for My strength
is made perfect in weakness.
2 CORINTHIANS 12:9

As you therefore have received Christ Jesus the Lord,
so walk in Him, rooted and built up
in Him and established in the faith.
COLOSSIANS 2:6-7

I thank Christ Jesus our Lord who has enabled me.
1 TIMOTHY 1:12

When I Need to Comfort Others

❧❧❧

LORD, THANK YOU FOR ALL YOU ARE DOING to enable my grief recovery. Now I am ready to be used by You in the lives of others who are suffering from one of the many forms of grief. Put these people on my agenda. Lead me to them. Give me an open, empathetic, and vulnerable spirit willing to share what You have taught me and the healing process through which You have led and continue to lead me.

As I have suffered grief, make me a "wounded healer." I have discovered that my own healing deepens as I care for others. I adopt Paul's prayer as my motto: "Blessed be the God and Father of our Lord Jesus, the Father of mercies and the God of all comfort, who comforts us in all our tribulation, that we may be able to comfort those who are in any trouble, with the comfort with which we ourselves are comforted by God" (2 Corinthians 1:3-4).

Help me remember that I didn't have to take grief alone. You sent me others who shared my grief, told me of how You helped them through their grief, and helped me turn my struggle into a stepping-stone. Lord, I don't want to do any less for the people around me who are suffering. And the wonder of it all is, the more I care for others, the stronger I become.

I've discovered how little people are prepared for the disappointments and discouragements that cause grief. So often they respond as if You are defeated by circumstance, rather than claiming Your power to defeat the enemy of death or the suffering of life. You, dear Christ, have won and are with me to help me claim Your victory. Amen.

It is interesting to note how the news of the outcome of the Battle of Waterloo was communicated to England. The message was sent by rider, by ship across the English Channel, and then by semaphore from ship to shore. The message had four words. Only the first two were communicated because a heavy fog descended suddenly. What got through was only, "W-e-l-l-i-n-g-t-o-n d-e-f-e-a-t-e-d." That's all the relay on the tower of Winchester Cathedral saw, and all he could do was pass on the sad news. England lived in disappointment for 24 hours.

Then the fog lifted, and the whole message could be completed. The two missing words hidden by the fog were, "t-h-e e-n-e-m-y."

Some of us face the loss of loved ones and our disappointments and discouragements with only half a message. We endure our grief as if Christ had been defeated rather than in the truth that Christ has defeated our enemies. At the death of a loved one, we think death has won. Not so for a Christian! Or in times of difficulty we sometimes live with half a message: a message of defeat.

The fog has lifted! Christ has won, and He is with us to help us claim His victory. Grief is the process during which His victory enables us to live again. There is life after grief. It's for you. It's for now. And it's yours to share with others.

PART III

In Times
of Pain

When I Endure
Physical Pain

◈

CHRIST, I CRY OUT TO YOU in times of physical pain. Bones ache, joints swell, nerves twitch with pulsating waves of pain. You know all about what I endure. It doesn't even compare with the anguish of Your suffering. But what I'm feeling is mine, in my body. I can't take it without the healing touch of Your hand. I yield my pain to You. Please, Lord, take it away, or give me the power to survive the devastating cause of it. I breathe out the pain and breathe in Your Spirit. Thank You for calming my panic.

I think of the time when four men tore a hole in the roof of a house in Capernaum where You were teaching. They lowered down a stretcher with their friend on it. Their deepest desire was to put the man face-to-face with You. I picture the moment his eyes met Yours and You reached out to touch and heal him.

I imagine myself on that stretcher being lowered down before You. Now I look into Your face: Wondrous love! I look into Your eyes: compassion, empathy, merciful care. And then I feel the healing hand. It's warm, tender, yet strong and powerful. I feel the surge of Your Spirit enter every facet of my being.

Lord, You are the Healer; You use medicine and doctors and nurses; You work through caregivers. And now I praise You that most of all You give Your healing touch when I need it so much! Amen.

The turning point in our healing often takes place when we surrender our plight to the Lord, relinquish our tenacious grip on our future, and relax in complete trust. Such a change releases all the potential healing resources of the body to be utilized by the Lord in getting well.

One of the reasons many of us miss that release of healing power is that we want to be sure of the results. So often we neglect bold prayers in Jesus' name, expecting His healing, because we are not sure He will act in the way we want, when we want it. The spirit of unbelief pervades our culture and infects our minds. Fear and panic about sickness make us helpless victims. We expect the worst and steel ourselves for its eventual occurrence.

Then in times of illness we realize how much we need the Lord's comfort and assurance. So we pray for His strength to endure. We are afraid to pray for healing because we fear we will be disappointed. Then where will we be? The last, frail thread of trust will be frayed and broken. That, too, is an effort to remain in charge, under our own control.

Putting our total life under the control of the Master is allowing Him to work out the results according to His plan. After all, we belong to Him whether we live or die. Death is a transition in the midst of eternal life. But in the meantime, the physical problems we face are to be committed to the Lord, placed under His authority, and released for His disposition as He deems best.

Christ is alive, present with us, and has the same authority He exercised over sickness when He was Jesus of Nazareth. Healing can be received to the fullest when we trust Him completely, believe all things are possible through Him, and allow Him to transform our thinking and our whole attitude toward life.

When I Need Peace
in the Midst of Pain

Dear Lord and Father of mankind,
Forgive our foolish ways...
Take from our souls the strain and stress,
And let our ordered lives confess
The beauty of Thy peace.

JOHN GREENLEAF WHITTIER

ᥩᥩᥩ

DEAR FATHER, THIS IS THE PEACE I need today. The conflict and tension of these days threaten to rob me of peace in my soul. It is easy to catch the emotional virus of frustration and exasperation, criticism and consternation, competition and quid-pro-quo manipulation.

Then I remember that Your peace is the healing antidote that can survive any circumstance. Give me the peace of a committed mind guided by Your Spirit and the peace that comes from trusting You. May Your deep peace flow into me, calming my impatience, and flow from me to others by my claiming Your inspiration. I hear the Prince of Peace whisper in my soul, "Peace I leave with you, My peace I give to you; not as the world gives do I give to you. Let not your heart be troubled, neither let it be afraid" (John 14:27).

Gracious Saviour, You are able to save to the uttermost those who come to You. By Your invitation and instigation, I come to You. You have encouraged me to ask for Your perfect peace in the midst of my pain. The fact of Your presence, the assurance of Your love, and the conviction that You are the healing power of the world give me the courage to ask You to deal with my pain in a way that is ultimately creative for me. Take it away, heal its causes, subdue its distressing discomfort, or simply give me strength to endure. When physical pain or the pain of heartache brings me to tears, quiet me in Your love and wipe away the tears from my eyes. Give me peace, dear Lord. Amen.

PRAYING THROUGH THE TOUGH TIMES

May the Lord of peace Himself give you
peace always in every way.

2 THESSALONIANS 3:16

Pursue peace with all people, and holiness,
without which no one will see the Lord.

HEBREWS 12:14

Brethren, whatever things are true, whatever things are
noble, whatever things are just, whatever things are pure,
whatever things are lovely, whatever things are of good report,
if there is any virtue and if there is anything praiseworthy—
meditate on these things. The things which you learned
and received and heard and saw in me, these do,
and the God of peace will be with you.

PHILIPPIANS 4:8-9

May the God of peace Himself sanctify you completely;
and may your whole spirit, soul and body be preserved
blameless at the coming of our Lord Jesus Christ.
He who calls you is faithful, who also will do it.

1 THESSALONIANS 5:23-24

When I Need God to Stay
My Mind on Him

꧁꧂

GRACIOUS GOD, YOU PROMISED through Isaiah that "You will keep him in perfect peace, whose mind is stayed on You, because he trusts in You" (Isaiah 26:3). I need this peace, the peace that passes understanding; the peace that settles my nerves and gives me serenity in these painful times. Your promise through Isaiah reminds me that You are the source of perfect peace, true *shalom/shalom*. You stay my mind on You— Your grace and goodness, Your faithfulness, Your resourcefulness, and Your forgiving heart.

Therefore, I commit all my cares and concerns to You. True peace can never be separated from Your Spirit. You are peace! Lasting peace is the result of a heart filled with Your Spirit of peace. Take up residence within me and spread Your peace to every facet of my being. Help me to receive Your gift of peace and hear your message in my soul. *"Shalom/shalom* to you today!" You say.

Dear God, show me what robs me of this wonderful gift. I really want to know, Father, so I can be specific in confession and commitment to change. May Your promises of peace in the Bible become real for me. You know how often I live with anxiety, frustration, and fear. In the quiet of this honest prayer, I open myself for You to teach me the secret of lasting peace. Thank You in advance for whatever it will take to help me receive Your peace so generously offered to me. In the name of the Prince of Peace. Amen.

Peace I leave with you, My peace I give to you;
not as the world gives do I give to you. Let not your heart
be troubled, neither let it be afraid.

JOHN 14:37

Let the peace of God rule in your hearts…Let the word
of Christ dwell in you richly in all wisdom.

COLOSSIANS 3:15-16

Having been justified by faith, we have peace
with God through our Lord Jesus Christ.

ROMANS 5:1

Grace to you and peace from God the Father
and our Lord Jesus Christ, who gave Himself for our sins,
that He might deliver us from this present evil age,
according to the will of our God and Father.

GALATIANS 1:3-4

It pleased the Father that in Him all the fullness should
dwell, and by Him to reconcile all things to Himself, by Him,
whether things on earth or in heaven, having made peace
through the blood of His cross. And you, who once
were alienated and enemies in your mind by wicked works,
yet now He has reconciled.

COLOSSIANS 1:19-21

When I Need Strength

⚬⚭⚬

THE PSALMIST REMINDS ME, "The LORD is my light and my salvation; whom shall I fear? The LORD is the strength of my life; of whom shall I be afraid?" (Psalm 27:1).

Dear God, grant me spiritual, intellectual, and physical revitalization today. You provide boundless energy when I am tense and tired. Your life force surges within me to give me enthusiasm for the work of this day and for the many challenges that I face. You lift out of my soul fear and panic, and in their place You put Your peace and power. Your love for me gives me a renewed desire to love and care for the people around me. Help me to give others the quality of kindness and patience and encouragement You have expressed to me. Saturate my soul with Your grace so that in spite of everything, joy might radiate on my face and be expressed in my attitude.

Astound me again with the magnitude of the responsibility You have given to me at this crucial time. Thank You for the moral and spiritual leadership You have called me to provide in my realm of responsibility. And so grant me special strength today; fill me with Your Spirit so that everything I say and do might glorify You. I count it a great blessing to be alive today and to be equipped by You to do, with inspired excellence, the work assigned to me. In the name of my dear Lord and Saviour. Amen.

He gives power to the weak, and to those who
have no might He increases strength.

ISAIAH 40:29

"Not by might nor by power, but by My Spirit,"
says the LORD of hosts.

ZECHARIAH 4:6

Most assuredly, I say to you, he who believes in Me,
the works that I do he will do also; and greater works
than these he will do, because I go to My Father.

JOHN 14:12

You shall receive power when the Holy Spirit
has come upon you; and you shall be witnesses to Me
in Jerusalem, and in all Judea and Samaria,
and to the end of the earth.

ACTS 1:8

For this reason I bow my knees to the Father of our Lord
Jesus Christ, from whom the whole family in heaven and
earth is named, that He would grant you, according to the
riches of His glory, to be strengthened with might through
His Spirit in the inner man, that Christ may dwell in your
hearts through faith; that you, being rooted and grounded in
love, may be able to comprehend with all the saints what is
the width and length and depth and height—to know the
love of Christ which passes knowledge; that you may be
filled with all the fullness of God.

Now to Him who is able to do exceedingly abundantly
above all that we ask or think, according to the power
that works in us, to Him be glory in the church
by Christ Jesus to all generations, forever and ever. Amen.

EPHESIANS 3:14-21

PRAYING THROUGH THE TOUGH TIMES

When I Face My Handicaps

〜✣〜

Gʀᴀᴄɪᴏᴜs Fᴀᴛʜᴇʀ, Yᴏᴜ ɢɪᴠᴇ ᴍᴇ inner eyes to see You and Your truth. Today I remember and celebrate the life of Helen Keller. Thank You for her courageous life. With Your help she overcame tremendous obstacles of being born blind and deaf. I am grateful for people like Anne Sullivan who taught her to read braille and helped her attend Radcliffe College and eventually become a prolific author.

My spirit is lifted today as I ponder Helen Keller's words, "I thank God for my handicaps, for, through them, I have found myself, my work and my God." I intentionally adopt for my life the four things Helen Keller urged people to learn in life: "To think clearly without hurry or confusion; to love everybody sincerely; to act in everything with the highest motives; to trust God unhesitantly." And for my work, Keller's words ring true: "Alone we can do so little; together we can do so much." Thank You, Father, for the memory of this great woman. Help me today to use all I have to do as much good as I can in as many circumstances and to as many people as I can.

Free me to face my own handicaps and overcome them with Your strength. Everyone has something that bogs him or her down at times. May the way I live through my own tough times help others I live with to have greater courage. Thank You, Lord, for making me a survivor! Amen.

The hands of those I meet are dumbly eloquent to me. I have met people so empty of joy that when I clasped their frosty fingertips it seemed as if I were shaking hands with a northeast storm. Others there are whose hands have sunbeams in them, so that their grasp warms my heart. It may be only the clinging touch of a child's hand, but there is as much potential sunshine in it for me as there is in a loving glance for others.

— *Helen Keller* —
from *The Story of My Life*

I can do all things through Christ who strengthens me.

PHILIPPIANS 4:13

I used to ask God to help me. Then I asked if I could help Him. I ended up by asking Him to do His work through me.

— *Hudson Taylor* —

Unless a man undertakes more than he possibly can do he will never do all he can do.

— *Henry Drummond* —

Things don't work out; God works out things!

— *Motto of Senator Max Cleland* —

who lost both legs and his right hand in Vietnam and is now a director of the Import–Export Bank of the United States

When I Need Courage

⸎

DEAR GOD, THANK YOU FOR ANOTHER DAY to live for Your glory by serving You. I accept the psalmist's admonition about You as my motto for the day: "Be of good courage, and He shall strengthen your heart" (Psalm 31:24). Your fresh supply of strength gives me courage to live fearlessly today. You replenish my diminished strength with intellectual creativity, emotional stability, and physical resilience. The tension of these frightening days on red alert have made me all the more alert to Your presence and power. The more I place my trust in You, the more the springs of tension within me are released and unwind until I feel a profound peace inside. I thank You for Your protection, and I renew my commitment to live by faith, not beset by fear. Your perfect love casts out fear.

Your grace and goodness give me stability and strength. Your fortitude surges into my heart. Your divine intelligence inspires my thinking. I will not be dismayed and cast about furtively for security in anything or anyone other than You. Fortified by Your power, help me to focus on the needs of others around me and in my community. May this be a truly great day as I serve You.

I relinquish my worries to You, and my anxiety is drained away. I say with the psalmist, "As for me, I trust You, O LORD; I say, 'You are my God.' My times are in Your hand" (Psalm 31:14-15). Amen.

From prayer that asks that I may be
Sheltered from winds that beat on Thee,
From fearing when I should aspire,
From faltering when I should climb higher,
From silken self, O Captain, free,
Thy soldier who would follow Thee.

From subtle love of softening things,
From easy choices, weakenings,
Not thus are spirits fortified,
Not this way went the Crucified,
From all that dims Thy Calvary,
O Lamb of God, deliver me.

Give me the love that leads the way,
The faith that nothing can dismay,
The hope no disappointments tire,
The passion that will burn like fire,
Let me not sink to be a clod:
Make me Thy fuel, Flame of God.

—*Amy Carmichael*—

When I Need to Overcome
Rather Than Be Overwhelmed

⊷⊶

LORD JESUS, WHAT YOU SAID to Your disciples on the night before Your crucifixion is the promise I want to claim for this day of my journey through difficult times: "In the world you have tribulation, but *take courage;* I have overcome the world (John 16:33 NASB). I hear You whisper in my soul, "Take courage! It's yours!" The imperative is bracing and stirring.

I know I can take hold of the gift of courage, because You have taken a hold of me. "Fear not, I am with you!" are Your courage-inducing words. Fear in these nerve-stretching days drives me to prayer. Courage displaces caution and reserve. I know that nothing can happen that will not bring me closer to You. What You give or withhold always is for my growth. My honest prayers are not an escape from reality and responsibility, but an encounter with them.

Thank You for courage that is based on convictions I cannot deny. You give me courage to act when I know what love demands. You energize my will to put into action costly obedience to You. Courage moves me from panic to Your perspective on things, and then to peace. Give me heightened awareness of what needs to be done, humble attentiveness to Your way to get it done, and honest accountability to You for faithful follow-through. Courage is the greatest virtue You give me because it makes possible all the rest. Today You will give me the power to overcome rather than be overwhelmed. Thank You, Lord!

It's not revolutions and upheavals that clear the road to new and better days, but someone's soul inspired and ablaze.

— Boris Pasternak —

To every man there openeth
A way, and ways and a way.
And the high soul climbs the high way
And the low soul gropes the low:
And in between, on the misty flats
The rest drift to and fro.
But to every man there openeth
A high way and a low
And every man decideth
The way his soul shall go.

— John Oxenham —

The Lord is constantly calling us out. He wants to get us to the place where He is our only security and assurance. Think of how hard we work to eliminate the risks of life. We labor, save, plan, and invest ourselves with safe responsibilities. Then we settle into the ruts of sameness and complain that life is no longer exciting.

As long as we are alive, there will be a next step in our adventure with the Lord. He constantly calls us out from where we are to a new level of risk. There will never be a time when what we've done or been can be our security. We were programmed to always be on the growing edge of new adventure. Where is the element of creative risk in your life? What would you do if you trusted God completely? Jim Elliot was right: "He is no fool who gives what he cannot keep to gain what he cannot lose."

When I Need Assurance in Unsure Times

❦❦❦

DEAR GOD, I AM PROFOUNDLY MOVED by Your merciful kindness to me. You never give up on me. When I forget You, You infuse my life with reminders of Your consistent love; when I resist Your guidance, You find new ways to get through to me; when hubris becomes a habit, You break the bond of self-sufficiency by showing me what I could accomplish with Your supernatural strength.

Lord, I confess my need for humility that is a combination of gratitude, honesty, and courage. I admit that all that I have and am is Your gift; I honestly face the distance between what I am and what I could be in my relationships and responsibilities; I need courage to blow the cap off of my reservations and live at full potential according to Your expectations.

Here I am at the beginning of another crucial day. As I rush into my schedule, I meet You at the pass. I don't need to spin to win with You. You know all about me. And so, I simply ask You to take my mind and focus my intelligence on what You will guide; to take my will and inspire me to choose what is righteous and just; and to take my voice and speak Your truth through it. Through Christ who is the way, the truth, and the life. Amen.

Yea, "new every morning," though we may awake,
Our hearts with old sorrow beginning to ache;
With old work unfinished when night stayed our hand,
When new duties waiting, unknown and unplanned;
With old care still pressing, to fret and to vex,
With new problems rising, our minds to perplex;
In ways long familiar, in paths yet untrod,
Oh, new every morning the mercies of God!

His faithfulness fails not; it meets each new day
With guidance for every new step of the way,
New grace for new trials, new trust for old fears,
New patience for bearing the wrongs of the years,
New strength for new burdens, new courage for old,
New faith for whatever the day may unfold;
As fresh for each need as the dew on the sod;
Oh, new every morning the mercies of God!

— *Annie Johnson Flint* —

PART IV

IN TIMES
OF PROBLEMS

When I Wonder If God Cares If I Have Problems

❦

Dear God, years of wrestling with problems have convinced me of a fact of life: I'm like most people in facing one momentous problem—the failure to understand that there is a positive and redemptive purpose to every one of the problems I face. I'm tempted to believe that there is something inherently bad about problems because they often involve me in an inconvenient interruption of my plans for a smooth and successful life.

Problems involve me in unpleasant pressures, distressing conflict, or in physical or emotional pain. I think that freedom from problems should be a reward for hard work, careful planning, and clear thinking. I struggle through the stages of life, battling the problems of getting an education, finding a job, developing a career, raising a family, making ends meet, and eventually retiring. At each stage I look forward to the next period as a time when the problems of life will be behind me. Most disturbing is the assumption that if I love You, commit my life to You, and diligently try to serve You, You will work things out so I don't have problems.

In this prayer, I want to separate myself from this crowd of people with these perceptions about problems. Your purposes are not thwarted by problems. I'm certain that when You allow a problem, it's because You want me to grow as a person. Actually, problems define the battle line of Your transforming encounter with ignorance, pride, selfishness, laziness, and resistance to growth. Problems help me reach out to You and allow You to help me find a creative solution and take the next step of becoming a more dynamic person. There's no problem too big for the two of us to solve together! Amen.

Make me a captive, Lord,
And then I shall be free;
Force me to render up my sword,
And I shall conqueror be.
I sink in life's alarms
When by myself I stand;
Imprison me within Thine arms,
And strong shall be my hand.

My heart is weak and poor
Until it master find;
It has no spring of action sure,
It varies with the wind.
It cannot freely move
Till Thou hast wrought its chain;
Enslave it with Thy matchless love,
And deathless it shall reign.

My will is not my own
Till Thou hast made it Thine;
If it would reach a monarch's throne
It must its crown resign;
It only stands unbent
Amid the clashing strife
When on Thy bosom it has leant,
And found in Thee its life.

—◦ *George Matheson* ◦—

When Life Doesn't Seem Fair

❧❧❧

$\mathcal{L}$ORD, IT'S WHEN THE SKY OF LIFE is covered with clouds that I do some hard thinking. I wrestle with the realization that often life doesn't seem fair. How could it be, in a deranged world where so few play by Your rules of righteousness and justice? But then I question my own shallow understanding of fairness: a happy, easy, problem-free, successful life. Is prosperity my divine right? Not when I review the Bible and Christian history. Some of the greatest women and men endured inexplicable suffering…and knew You more intimately because of it than those who tried to demand that You produce what they wanted, when they wanted it.

The clouds of unknowing still cover the sky. I've known physical pain sometimes; other times, guilt or grief; still other times, emotional hurts, lurking memories, worry over others, anxiety about the future. Pain, nonetheless.

And yet, dear loving Lord, You've helped me discover a liberating truth: When the storm clouds bring me to a realization of how much I need You, and I cry out to You and thank You for reaching across my imagined breach of separation from You, You assure me of Your love and help me make a fresh start. Then I hear You say, "I will never forget You; I remember my covenant; you belong to Me!"

The clouds of doubt, fear, and anxiety break; the sun shines again. The heavy black clouds that once blocked the sun have slowly disappeared, sprinkling their last little showers. Good things are coming! And the final raindrops after the storm serve the sun in producing a rainbow, the sign of the covenant! Amen.

God's Rainbow

Ye fearful saints, fresh courage take;
The clouds ye so much dread
Are filled with mercy and shall break
In blessings on your head.

—◦ *William Cowper* ◦—

I set My rainbow in the cloud, and it shall be for the sign
of the covenant between Me and the earth. It shall be,
when I bring a cloud over the earth, that the rainbow
shall be seen in the cloud; and I will remember My
covenant which is between Me and you…The rainbow
shall be in the cloud, and I will look on it to remember
the everlasting covenant.

GENESIS 9:13-15

What skillful limner e'er would choose
To paint the rainbow's varying hues
Unless to mortal it were given
To dip his brush in the dyes of heaven?

—◦ *Sir Walter Scott* ◦—

O Joy that seekest me through pain
I cannot close my heart to Thee
I climb the rainbow through the rain
And feel the promise is not vain
That morn shall tearless be.

—◦ *George Matheson* ◦—

The word *covenant* means an irrevocable bond. God has
pledged Himself to how He will deal with us. He will not
forget His promise He has made to be merciful, gracious,
and kind.

When I Feel Empty

❧❧❧

GRACIOUS LORD, I CONFESS THE BURDENS I have tried to carry myself: personal needs, physical tiredness, weariness of living on my own strength, anxiety for the suffering people endure, discouragement in renewing the tradition-bound church, frustration in caring for religious people who may not know You, and anguish over the battle for justice and righteousness in culture. I come empty to be filled, humanly inadequate to be anointed with gifts beyond my talents: a riverbed ready to receive the flow of Your supernatural power. Thank You for loving me as I am, but not leaving me there. Help me press on to live with greater passion than ever before.

You have shown me that the antidote to pride is praise. In this time of prayer, I intentionally praise You for all that I might be tempted to think I have achieved on my own. Pride stunts my spiritual growth and makes me a difficult person for You to bless. Forgive me when I grasp the glory for myself. Thank You for breaking the bubble of the illusion that I am where I am because of my own cleverness or cunning. Humbly I acknowledge that I could not think a creative thought without Your inspiration and guidance, or accomplish anything of lasting value without Your power and courage. Amen.

Even to your old age, I am He, and even to gray hairs
I will carry you! I have made, and I will bear;
even I will carry, and will deliver you.

May our Lord Jesus Christ Himself, and our God and
Father, who has loved us and given us everlasting
consolation and good hope by grace, comfort your hearts
and establish you in every good word and work.

2 THESSALONIANS 2:16-17

His lord said to him, "Well done, good and faithful servant;
you were faithful over a few things, I will make you ruler
over many things. Enter into the joy of your lord." He also
who had received two talents came and said, "Lord, you
delivered to me two talents; look, I have gained two more
talents besides them." His lord said to him, "Well done,
good and faithful servant; you were faithful over a few
things, I will make you ruler over many things.
Enter into the joy of your lord."

MATTHEW 25:21-23

Be steadfast, immovable, always abounding
in the work of the Lord, knowing that
your labor is not in vain in the Lord.

1 CORINTHIANS 15:58

PRAYING THROUGH THE TOUGH TIMES

When Problems Pile Up

❧⸱❧

Lord, You know that problems have a way of piling up. They accumulate—and suddenly, too many surface at the same time. Sometimes it's my own fault. I've neglected lots of potential problems, saying, "I'll worry about that tomorrow"…or I put off doing the caring thing for the people in my life…or sometimes they all want my attention at the same time.

But what are You trying to teach me, Lord? I sit here in the quiet, and Your answers begin to flow. Help me meditate on the steps You give me so I don't forget them. I'm listening, Lord.

1. *Focus on You, not the circumstances.* I will deliberately turn my eyes away from the problems. This will release me from the tension of trying to solve the problems on my own strength.

2. *Now face the problem.* So many problems engulf me before I take a good look at them. You will show me what You want me to learn and discover a potential good wrapped inside the problem.

3. *Thank You.* Thanksgiving affirms that I know You care and will use the problem for my growth and Your purposes. Problems are an occasion for deeper trust and progress.

4. *Put blame behind me.* When a problem hits, it doesn't make much difference who caused it. I won't blame anyone, not even myself. If I caused it, I will confess it, accept forgiveness, and get on with allowing You to guide me to creative solutions.

5. *Commit the problem to You in prayer.* That will open the floodgates for the flow of Your wisdom into my mind.

6. *Claim Your promise to help me.* I am not alone.

7. *Share the problem with trusted friends.* You will use them to communicate Your insight and guidance.

8. *Take the first step.* You will show me the first step. I won't be able to take subsequent steps until I make the initial move. Obedience is the key to spiritual knowledge and the further release of power for subsequent steps. You will give me the goal and vision of the solution according to Your plan. Then You will give me the courage to get moving under Your direction.

Thank You, Lord, for these practical steps. I hear You! Amen.

How precious are Your thoughts to me, O God!
How great is the sum of them!

PSALM 139:17

Show me Your Ways, O LORD;
Teach me Your paths.
Lead me in Your truth and teach me,
For You are the God of my salvation;
On You I wait all the day.

PSALM 25:4-5

Ask and it will be given to you; seek and you will find; knock and the door will be opened to you. For everyone who asks receives; he who seeks finds; and to him who knocks, the door will be opened.

Which of you, if his son asks for bread, will give him a stone? Or if he asks for a fish, will give him a snake? If you, then, though you are evil, know how to give good gifts to your children, how much more will your Father in heaven give good gifts to those who ask Him!

MATTHEW 7:7-11

When I'm Blessed to Have Problems

STRONG, PROBLEM-SOLVING LORD, there is so much in life I can't be sure of, but Your Word trumpets a truth I can count on: Irrespective of the intensity of my problems, You, the Lord of all creation, are with me. In fact, You've helped me believe that my problems can be proof of Your recreating presence. You allow problems to perk to the surface because You are ready to deal with them through me.

I'm blessed to have problems! You have decided not to leave me where I am. You've willed to change things, You're on the move calling me to face relational difficulties, You're helping me understand why some people are so difficult, You're giving me wisdom to unravel family problems that have kept me from deeper experiences of oneness with loved ones. You also call me into cultural battles for truth and righteousness. So, in reality, a good test of how alive I am is how many soul-sized problems You have allowed me to tackle with Your power and guidance.

The bigger the problem, the more of Your abiding presence I will receive. The more complex the problem, the more advanced will be the wisdom You offer. Equal to the strain of the problem will be the strength that You release. Now I know the hidden truth! It is an evidence of Your presence that You allow problems...to focus the next step of what You want to accomplish in my own life, and accomplish through me in my significant relationships, in my friends, at work, in my church, and in our culture.

I will always have problems. That's life. But I also have You, Lord, who will not only help me grow through them but will give me the power to triumph over them. Amen.

The Lord is righteous in all His ways,
Gracious in all His works.
The Lord is near to all who call upon Him,
To all who call upon Him in truth.
He will fulfill the desire of those who fear Him;
He also will hear their cry and save them.

PSALM 145:17-19

May our Lord Jesus Christ Himself, and our God the Father,
who has loved us and given us everlasting consolation and
good hope by grace, comfort your hearts and establish you
in every good word and work.

2 THESSALONIANS 2:16-17

The weapons of our warfare are not carnal
but mighty in God for pulling down strongholds,
casting down arguments and every high thing that
exalts itself against the knowledge of God, bringing
every thought into captivity to the obedience of Christ.

2 CORINTHIANS 10:4-5

Take up the whole armor of God, that you may be able
to withstand in the evil day, and having done all, to stand.
Stand therefore, having girded your waist with truth,
having put on the breastplate of righteousness, and having
shod your feet with the preparation of the gospel of peace;
above all, taking the shield of faith with which you will
be able to quench all the fiery darts of the wicked one.
And take the helmet of salvation, and the
sword of the Spirit, which is the word of God.

EPHESIANS 6:13-17

PRAYING THROUGH THE TOUGH TIMES

When I Am Rushed and Pressured

God is love, and he who abides in love abides in God, and God in him.

1 JOHN 4:16

❧❧❧

GRACIOUS GOD, THANK YOU FOR INSPIRING John so many years ago to write what I am feeling today. In this time of quiet, I want to abide in Your presence. Even now I feel my tensions melt away. My fears are invaded by Your love, and my hopes are maximized by Your vision of what You are able and ready to do today. Help me to abound in the unsearchable riches of Your limitless resources. Go before me to show the way, and help me to anticipate and joyously receive the amazing gifts of love You prepared for me long before I dared to ask. In the rush and pressure of this day, keep me in the abiding place of power.

Lord, You know better than I do what I am facing today. I surrender all my hopes and dreams, plans, and visions to Your perfect will. I want to do what You want me to do. I've learned that that's the only source of Your gift of guidance. Thank You for the gift today. I know You will be with me. That's all I need to know.

Gracious Lord of history, I praise You that my times are in Your hand. You know the end from the beginning, blessed Alpha and Omega. Having settled the issue of the end of time, I long to accomplish Your ends in time. Thank You for helping me maximize my hours. Help me to be fully present to You and to people, as well as to all the delights and difficulties You will use for Your glory and my growth. Through Christ my Lord. Amen.

My Shepherd

The Lord will work for me!
The LORD is my shepherd;
I shall not want.

The Lord will provide for me!
He makes me to lie down in green pastures;
He leads me beside the still waters.

The Lord will keep me going!
He restores my soul.

The Lord will guide me!
He leads me in the paths of righteousness
For His name's sake.

The Lord will protect me!
Yea, though I walk through the valley of the shadow of death,
I will fear no evil;
For You are with me;
Your rod and Your staff, they comfort me.

The Lord will heal me!
You prepare a table before me in the presence of my enemies;
You anoint my head with oil;
My cup runs over.

The Lord will pursue me!
Surely goodness and mercy shall follow me
All the days of my life;
And I will dwell in the house of the LORD
Forever.

—⁂ *Lloyd John Ogilvie* ⁂—

When I Need to See the Way

Trust in the LORD *with all your heart,*
And lean not on your own understanding;
In all your ways acknowledge Him,
And He shall direct your paths.

PROVERBS 3:5-6

❦❦❦

O GOD, WHO IN THE WORK OF CREATION commanded light
to shine out of darkness, shine in my mind. You have given me
the gift of intellect to think things through in the light of Your
guidance. Dispel the darkness of doubt and the petulance of
prejudice so I may know what righteousness and justice
demand. I pray with Søren Kierkegaard, "Give us weak eyes
for things which are of no account and clear eyes for all Your
truth."

I seek Your truth in the issues before me. Place in my mind
clear discernment of what is Your will for me. May I constantly pray with the psalmist, "Lead me, O LORD, in Your
righteousness...make Your way straight before my face"
(Psalm 5:8). Help me to look ahead to every detail of the day
and picture You guiding my steps, shaping my attitudes,
inspiring my thoughts, and enabling abundant living. May
the vision You guide be equaled by the momentary power You
provide. Give me wisdom to perceive You, diligence to seek
You, patience to wait for You, a heart to receive You, and the
opportunity to serve You.

Gracious God, I put my trust in You. I resist the human
tendency to lean on my own understanding; I acknowledge
my need for Your wisdom in my search for solutions in my
tough times. As an intentional act of will, I commit to You
everything I think, say, and do today. Direct my paths as I
give precedence to loyalty to You over anything or anyone else.
I need You, Father. Amen.

If you abide in My word, you are
My disciples indeed. And you shall know the truth,
and the truth shall make you free.

JOHN 8:31-32

Your kingdom come. Your will be done
on earth as it is in heaven.

MATTHEW 6:10

I delight to do Your will, O my God,
And Your law is within my heart.

PSALM 40:8

I have taught you in the way of wisdom;
I have led you in right paths.

PROVERBS 4:11

I will bless the LORD who has given me counsel;
My heart also instructs me in the night seasons.
I have set the LORD always before me;
Because He is at my right hand I shall not be moved.

PSALM 16:7-8

Come now, you who say, "Today or tomorrow we will go to
such and such a city, spend a year there, buy and sell, and
make a profit"; whereas you do not know what will happen
tomorrow. For what is your life? It is even a vapor that
appears for a little time and then vanishes away. Instead you
ought to say, "If the Lord wills, we shall live and do this
or that." But now you boast in your arrogance. All such
boasting is evil. Therefore, to him who knows to do good
and does not do it, to him it is sin.

JAMES 4:13-17

When I Need Confidence in Problems

ALMIGHTY GOD, I CLAIM YOUR PROMISE through Jeremiah: "Call to Me, and I will answer you, and show you great and mighty things, which you do not know" (Jeremiah 33:3). I press on with confidence to the challenges ahead today. Irrespective of perplexities, You are with me. The bigger the problems, the more of Your power I will receive. The more complex the issues, the more wisdom You will offer. Equal to the strain will be the strength You grant me.

So, I humble myself and confess my need for Your divine inspiration. My experience, education, and expertise are insufficient to grasp the full potential of Your vision for my life and the world. I need Your X-ray discernment into potential blessings wrapped up in what I often call problems. Endow me with wisdom to see clearly the solutions I could not discover without Your help. Give me courage to seek and follow Your guidance. Set my heart on fire with greater patriotism for our country and a deeper dedication to be a courageous problem-solver for Your glory and by Your grace.

Thank you for family and friends who depend on me. Help me communicate Your love, forgiveness, peace, and hope. Sometimes I get exasperated at what they do or say. It's hard to keep on loving when I feel rejection or lack of respect. I want to cry out, "Lord, get me out of this!" rather than asking, "Lord, what do you want me to get out of this?" Help me overcome the illusion that the only time You are present is when everything is going smoothly. You are my triumphant Lord in tough times. Amen.

This is the confidence that we have in Him, that if we ask anything according to His will, He hears us. And if we know that He hears us, whatever we ask, we know that we have the petitions that we have asked of Him.

1 JOHN 5:14-15

We share in Christ, if only we hold
our first confidence firm to the end.

HEBREWS 3:14 RSV

Our confidence in Christ does not make us lazy, negligent or careless, but on the contrary, it awakens us, urges on, and makes us active in living righteous lives and doing good. There is no self-confidence to compare with it. I have one passion: It is He! It is He!

— *Ulrich Zwingli* —

We have a great need for Christ and we have a great Christ for our needs.

— *C.H. Spurgeon* —

When I Am Weary

❧❧❧

ALMIGHTY GOD, REIGN SUPREME as sovereign Lord in my life today. Enter my mind and heart and show me the way. May I be given supernatural insight and wisdom to discern Your guidance each step of the way through this challenging day. Break deadlocks with people, enable creative compromises, and inspire a spirit of unity. Overcome the weariness of hard work. Give me a second wind to press on.

When there is nowhere else to turn in my human dilemmas and difficulties, it is time to return to You. When I fail to work things out, I must ask You to work out things. When my burdens make me downcast, I cast my burdens on You. If You could create the universe and uphold it with Your providential care, You can solve my most complex problems.

Dear Father, I want to know You so well, trust You so completely, seek Your wisdom so urgently, and receive Your inspiration so intentionally that I will be a person totally available for the influence of Your Spirit. Help me to be just as receptive to Your direction. Alarm me with disquiet in my soul if what I plan is less than Your best. With equal force confirm any conviction that will move forward what You think is best for me. Remind me that You are with me and will guide me. You are Jehovah-Shammah: You will be there! Amen.

I will lift up my eyes to the hills—
From whence comes my help?
My help comes from the LORD,
Who made heaven and earth.

He will not allow your foot to be moved;
He who keeps you will not slumber.
Behold, He who keeps Israel
Shall neither slumber nor sleep.

The LORD is your keeper;
The LORD is your shade at your right hand.
The sun shall not strike you by day,
Nor the moon by night.

The LORD shall preserve you from all evil;
He shall preserve your soul.
The LORD shall preserve your going out and your coming in
From this time forth, and even forevermore.

PSALM 121

Why are you cast down, O my soul?
And why are you disquieted within me?
Hope in God;
For I shall yet praise Him,
The help of my countenance and my God.

PSALM 42:11

When I Need to Be Expectant

❧❧❧

Almighty God, Your intervention in trying times in the past has made me an experienced optimist for the future. My confidence is rooted in Your reliability. You are with me; therefore I will not fear. Your commandments give me Your absolutes; therefore I will not waver. You call me to obey You as well as love You; therefore I will not compromise my convictions.

You will give me strength and courage for each challenge; therefore I will not be anxious. You have called me to glorify You with my work; therefore I will seek to do everything with excellence. You have inspired me to be merciful as You are merciful; therefore I will refrain from condemnatory judgments. You have helped me through contentious times of discord and disunity in the past; therefore I ask for Your help for today as I wait for the resolution of those problems I have placed in Your hands.

My loving Lord, I listen intently to Your assurance spoken through Jeremiah: "I have loved you with an everlasting love; therefore with lovingkindness I have drawn you" (Jeremiah 31:3). These amazing words resound in my soul. Can they be true? Your grace is indefatigable. It is magnetic. You draw me to Yourself, and I receive strength and hope. I am secure in You and therefore can live and work with freedom and joy. I know Your absolutes are as irrevocable as Your love is irresistible. Now I have the strength to live Your commandments for abundant life—"Choose this day whom you will serve," and Jesus' mandate, "Set your mind on God's Kingdom...before everything else!" (Matthew 6:33 NEB). In His powerful name. Amen.

When God wants to drill a person,
And skill a person,
And thrill a person,
When God wants to mold a person
To play the noblest part,
When He yearns with all His heart
To create so great and bold a person
That all the world will be amazed,
Watch His methods, watch His ways
How He persistently perfects
Whom He royally elects
How He bends but never breaks
When His good He undertakes
How He uses whom He chooses
And with every crisis fuses
And by every blessing induces
To try His splendor out.
God knows what He's about.
His promises are true.
God has plans for you!

Anonymous

When I Need
Supernatural Insight

❦❧❦❧

$\mathcal{G}$RACIOUS FATHER, LORD OF the ups and downs of life, Lord of the seeming triumphs and supposed disappointments, Lord who does not change in the midst of change, I come to You for Your strength and Your power. Make me a hopeful person who expects great strength from You and continues to attempt great strategies for You. Replenish me with your strength so that I may soar. I claim Your promise through Isaiah—"Those who wait on the LORD shall renew their strength; they shall mount up with wings like eagles, they shall run and not be weary, they shall walk and not faint" (Isaiah 40:31).

You have called me to be a creative thinker. I begin this day by yielding my thinking brain to Your magnificent creativity. You know everything, You also know what is best for me, and You have entrusted me with responsibilities. I am grateful that You not only are omniscient, but also omnipresent. You are here with me now and will be with me wherever this day's responsibilities take me. I take seriously the admonition of Proverbs 16:3, "Commit your works to the LORD, and your thoughts will be established."

Thank You for this secret of success in Your Word. In response I look to what is ahead this day and thank You in advance for supernatural intelligence to maximize my thinking. You are my Lord and Saviour. Amen.

If you receive my words, and treasure my commands
within you, that you incline your ear to wisdom,
and apply your heart to understanding;
yes, if you cry out for discernment, and lift up your voice
for understanding, if you seek her as silver,
and search for her as for hidden treasures; then you will
understand the fear of the LORD, and find the knowledge of
God. For the LORD gives wisdom; from His mouth
come knowledge and understanding.

PROVERBS 2:1-6

That which was from the beginning, which we have heard,
which we have seen with our eyes, which we have
looked upon, and our hands have handled, concerning the
Word of life—the life was manifested, and we have seen, and
bear witness and declare to you that eternal life which was
with the Father and was manifested to us—that which we
have seen and heard we declare to you, that you also may
have fellowship with us; and truly our fellowship is with the
Father and with His Son Jesus Christ. And these things
we write to you that your joy may be full.

1 JOHN 1:1-4

We...do not cease to pray for you, and to ask that you may
be filled with the knowledge of His will in all wisdom and
spiritual understanding; that you may walk worthy of the
Lord, fully pleasing Him, being fruitful in every
good work and increasing in the knowledge of God;
strengthened with all might, according to His glorious
power, for all patience and longsuffering with joy.

COLOSSIANS 1:9-11

PRAYING THROUGH THE TOUGH TIMES

When I Need Joy in Trials

ᴄᴏ᚛᚜᚛᚜᚛ᴏ

*J*OYOUS GOD, IN WHOSE HEART FLOWS limitless joy, I come to You to receive Your artesian joy. You have promised joy to those who know You intimately, who trust You completely, and who serve You by caring for the needs of others. I agree with Robert Louis Stevenson, "To miss the joy is to miss everything."

And yet, I confess that often I do miss the joy You offer. It is so much more than happiness, which is dependent on people, circumstances, and keeping things under my control. Sometimes I become grim. I take myself too seriously and don't take Your grace seriously enough. Give me the psalmist's assurance about You when he said, "God my exceeding joy"; or Nehemiah's confidence, "The joy of the LORD" is my strength; or Jesus' secret of lasting joy: abiding in Your love.

Grant me fresh joy in my trials. I can take most anything when Your grace produces joy in spite of how tough things get. Thank You for James' bracing word, "Count it all joy when you fall into various trials, knowing that the testing of your faith produces patience. But let patience have its perfect work, that you may be perfect and complete, lacking in nothing" (James 1:2-4).

May this be a day when I serve You with gladness because Your joy has filled my heart. Through Christ, who has promised me His joy! Amen.

Restore to me the joy of Your salvation,
and uphold me by Your generous Spirit.

PSALM 51:12

I will rejoice in the LORD, I will joy in the God of my
salvation. The LORD God is my strength; He will make
my feet like deer's feet, and He will make me walk
on my high hills.

HABAKKUK 3:18-19

Oh come, let us sing to the LORD! Let us shout joyfully to
the Rock of our salvation. Let us come before His presence
with thanksgiving; let us shout joyfully to Him with psalms.

PSALM 95:1-2

May the God of hope fill you with all joy
and peace in believing, that you may abound
in hope by the power of the Holy Spirit.

ROMANS 15:13

I will greatly rejoice in the LORD, my soul shall be joyful
in my God; for He has clothed me with the garments
of salvation, He has covered me with the robe of
righteousness, as a bridegroom decks himself with
ornaments, and as a bride adorns herself with her jewels.

ISAIAH 61:10

Until now you have asked nothing in My name.
Ask, and you will receive, that your joy may be full.

JOHN 16:24

...that I may finish my race with joy.

ACTS 20:24

PRAYING THROUGH THE TOUGH TIMES

When I Am Under Stress

❧❧❧

LORD, I NEED YOUR HELP. I am feeling the strain of stress. My body is agitated by worry and fear. I confess to You my inability to handle it alone. I surrender my mind to You. Take charge of the control center of my brain. Think Your thoughts through me, and send into my nervous system the pure signals of Your peace, power, and patience. I don't want to have a divided mind fractured off from Your control.

Forgive my angers rooted in petulant self-will. Make me a channel, a riverbed, of Your love to others suffering as much stress as I. Help me act on the inspiration You give me rather than stifling Your guidance.

Take charge of my tongue so it becomes an instrument of healing. Make me a communicator of love and forgiveness as I cheer others on to their best.

I commit my schedule to You, Lord—help me to know and do Your will. Guide me in doing Your will on Your timing so I don't burn out doing the things I don't really want to do, or fear to do what is Your best for me. Set me free from the tyranny of acquisitiveness and the lust of seeking my security in things rather than in my relationship with You.

I long to be the person You created me to be, and not anyone else. Forgive me when I take my signals of success from others and not You.

Most of all, Lord, help me to catch the drumbeat of Your guidance and live by Your timing. Here is my life—invade it, fill it, transform it. And I thank You in advance for the healing of my life and for giving me strength to conquer stress. Amen.

Ten Things I Will Do to Realize
the Lord's Healing of Stress

1. I recognize that stress is a major problem in my life.

2. I praise the Lord for the magnificent stress-coping mechanism He has given me.

3. I acknowledge the linkage between my thinking and attitudes and my body's stress-producing systems.

4. I am thankful that my body can produce energy to assist me in meeting life's demands, challenges, and opportunities.

5. I seek to yield my thinking brain to the conditioning and control of the indwelling Christ.

6. I will set aside a time each day for meditation so that Christ can guide my thoughts and attitudes, decisions and actions, relationships and responsibilities.

7. I will quickly admit my inadequacy to manage stress and will talk to trusted confidants, fellow stress-strugglers, to release the build-up of stress and receive from them encouragement and prayer.

8. I will be as honest as I can be about how stress is affecting my life and what my attitudes may be doing to cause it.

9. I will pray daily for other sufferers of stress, claiming Christ's healing power for them.

10. I will be sensitive to the things I do and say that cause stress in the people in my life—and will, whenever possible, work to bring changes in the institutions, organizations, and groups of which I am a part in order to diffuse the stress-inducing culture in our country today.

When I Need a Gift of Enthusiasm

❦

O Christ of spiritual fire, set me aflame with true passion. Your presence burning in me gives me empathy for others and enthusiasm for my calling to be your disciple. Your love in me is like a fire. It sets me ablaze with moral passion and social responsibility. You give me devotion for social justice. My commitment to fight for what is right consumes me. On fire with patriotism, I love my nation and serve with radiance. Your fire also burns out the chaff of negativism, divisiveness, and judgmentalism. You purify my motives with Your holy fire.

Lord, Your fire galvanized me into oneness with other believers. Here is my heart. If it has burned out, relight it; if the flame is low, stoke it with Your Spirit; if my fires are banked, set them ablaze again.

Source of strength to live life to the fullest, replenish my enthusiasm for the people of my life, the work You have given me to do, and the leadership I must provide. What Vesuvius would be without fire, or Niagara without water, or the firmament without the sun, so I would be without enthusiasm. But Lord, You know what happens to me in the pressures and problems of life. The ruts of sameness become well-worn; the blight of boredom settles on the bloom of what was once thrilling. I know I need a fresh gift of enthusiasm when prayer becomes routine, or people are taken for granted, or reading Scripture or singing praises does not send a thrill up my spine, or the privilege of living in this free land becomes mundane.

Give me a burst of enthusiasm for the privilege of being alive. Renew my awe and wonder, my vision and hope, and my sense of gratitude that You have chosen to be my Lord and have chosen me to love and serve You. Set me ablaze, Lord! Amen.

He will baptize you with the Holy Spirit and fire.

LUKE 3:16

As it is written: "Eye has not seen, nor ear heard, nor have entered into the heart of man the things which God has prepared for those who love Him." But God has revealed them to us through His Spirit. For the Spirit searches all things, yes, the deep things of God...Now we have received, not the spirit of the world, but the Spirit who is from God, that we might know the things that have been freely given to us by God.

These things we also speak, not in words which man's wisdom teaches but which the Holy Spirit teaches, comparing spiritual things with spiritual. But the natural man does not receive the things of the Spirit of God, for they are foolishness to him; nor can he know them, because they are spiritually discerned. But he who is spiritual judges all things, yet he himself is rightly judged by no one. For "who has known the mind of the LORD that he may instruct Him?" But we have the mind of Christ.

1 CORINTHIANS 2:9-16

When He, the Spirit of truth, has come,
He will guide you into all truth; for He will not speak on His own authority, but whatever He hears He will speak; and He will tell you things to come. He will glorify Me, for He will take of what is Mine and declare it to you. All things that the Father has are Mine. Therefore I said that He will take of Mine and declare it to you.

JOHN 16:13

The supreme need of the church is the same in the twentieth century as in the first; it is men and women on fire for Christ.

—◦ *James S. Stewart* ◦—

When I Need God's Blessing

The LORD bless you and keep you;
The LORD make His face to shine upon you,
And be gracious to you;
The LORD lift up His countenance upon you,
And give you peace.

NUMBERS 6:24-26

ᏬᏇᏋᏇᎧ

FATHER, I BEGIN THIS DAY BY CLAIMING this magnificent five-fold assurance. I ask You to make this a blessed day, filled with the assurance of Your blessings. May I live today with the godly esteem of knowing You have chosen me and called me to receive Your love and to serve You. Keep me safe from danger and the forces of evil. Give me the helmet of salvation to protect my thinking brain from any intrusion of temptation to pride, resistance to Your guidance, or negative attitudes. Smile on me as Your face, Your presence, lifts me from fear and frustration.

Thank You for Your grace to overcome the grimness that sometimes pervades my countenance. Instead, may my face reflect Your joy. May Your peace flow into me, calming my agitated spirit, conditioning my disposition, and controlling all I say and do. Help me to say to people, "Have a blessed day," and expect nothing less for myself.

Before me is a brand-new day filled with opportunities to live out my calling to love others. I trust You to guide me so that all that I do and say today will be for Your glory.

Since I will pass through this life only once, if there is any kindness I can express, any affirmation I can communicate, any help I can give, free me to do it today. Help me to be sensitive to what is happening to people around me. May I take no one for granted, but instead, be a communicator of Your love and encouragement. Amen.

What then shall we say to these things ? If God is for us, who can be against us? He who did not spare His own Son, but delivered Him up for us all, how shall He not with Him also freely give us all things? Who shall bring a charge against God's elect? It is God who justifies. Who is he who condemns? It is Christ who died, and furthermore is also risen, who is even at the right hand of God, who also makes intercession for us. Who shall separate us from the love of Christ? Shall tribulation, or distress, or persecution, or famine, or nakedness, or peril, or sword?…

Yet in all these things we are more than conquerors through Him who loved us. For I am persuaded that neither death nor life, nor angels nor principalities nor powers, nor things present nor things to come, nor height nor depth, nor any other created thing, shall be able to separate us from the love of God which is in Christ Jesus our Lord.

ROMANS 8:31-35,37-39

When I Need Christ-Esteem

Give, and it will be given to you: good measure, pressed down, shaken together, and running over will be put into your bosom. For with the measure that you use, it will be measured back to you.

LUKE 6:38

꧁꧂

DEAR CHRIST, WHO HAS GRACIOUSLY MADE every person a never-to-be-repeated miracle of uniqueness, I praise You that I can be myself because You love me, I can use my gifts because You gave them to me, and I can grasp the opportunities You provide because You want to surprise me with Your goodness. All I possess and have become is because of Your Providence. The wonder of it all is that it is Your nature to go beyond what You have done before. This gives the zest of expectation and excitement to my life. It also helps me know I can come to You with my worries and anxieties, my fears and frustrations, my hopes and hurts.

You know me as I really am and see beneath the shining armor of pretended sufficiency. You know when I am at the end of my tether and need Your strength; You understand my discouragements and disappointments and renew my hope; You feel my physical and emotional pain and heal me. You have told me that to whom much is given, of that one much will be required. Thank You that You have also taught me that to the one of whom much is required, much shall be given. Help me to be a grateful receiver. Amen.

Jesus Christ, in His infinite love, became what we are in order that He might make us who He wholly is.

— *Irenaeus* —

He became what we are that He might make us what He is.

— *Athanasius* —

We shall be like Him, for we shall see Him as He is.

1 JOHN 3:2

The good toward which all things work together is that we are conformed to the image of Christ.

— *G. Campbell Morgan* —

Robert Rainy, the Scottish divine, closed a communion meditation by leaning across the communion table and flinging out this challenge: "Do you believe your faith? Do you believe this I'm telling you? Do you believe a day is coming, really coming, when you will stand before the throne of God, and the angels will whisper together and say, 'Oh, how like Jesus Christ he is?' Do you hear the whisper? You don't have to wait…heaven has begun. How like Christ you are becoming!"*

---

* Quoted by Arthur John Gossip, *From the Edge of the Crowd* (Edinburgh: T&T. Clark, 1924), p. 12.

When I Need Christ's Hand
on My Shoulder

When I saw Him, I fell at His feet as dead. But He laid His right hand on me, saying to me, "Do not be afraid; I am the First and the Last. I am He who lives, and was dead, and behold, I am alive forevermore. Amen."

REVELATION 1:17-18

GRACIOUS LORD CHRIST, THANK YOU for Your hand upon my shoulder assuring me of Your providential, palpable presence and reminding me of Your power. It is a hand of comfort as You tell me again that You will be with me regardless of what happens. It is a hand of conscription calling me to be an "aye ready!" servant who has received from You the orders of the day. It is a hand of courage that gives me daring to take action because You have taken hold of me. It is a hand of correction alerting me to what may be less than Your best for me, or my loved ones and friends. It is a hand of confidence to press forward. Your faithfulness fails not; it meets the problems of today with fresh guidance for each step of the way. So I will be all the bolder; Your hand is upon my shoulder. I will not waiver; You are my Lord and Saviour. Amen.

All of life will be a successive series of astonishments with what Christ is able and ready to do through intervening love. His "Lo, I am with you always" becomes the basis of a sensitized recognition of His breakthrough into our problems. When we least expect it, He is there. When we are not aware of His presence, He gives us what we need. There are times when the language of the old gospel song alone suffices— "Hallelujah! What a Savior!"

Suddenly all of life is alive with Christ. What we need is what Newman called a "wise receptivity."

I have come to believe that an outward evidence of the indwelling of Christ is the capacity constantly to be astonished at what He is up to in our lives. A bored, bland, unsurprisable, unamazed Christian is a contradiction of terms. My prayer is, "O Christ, keep me sensitive to see You alive in the world around me, active in the lives of people, and abundant in unexpected blessings."

Saul Kane expressed that kind of astonishment after his conversion in John Masefield's poem "The Everlasting Mercy."

> The station brook, to my new eyes
> Was babbling out of Paradise.
> The waters rushing from the rain
> Were singing Christ has risen again.
> I thought all earthly creatures knelt
> From rapture of the joy I felt.

When I Need Wisdom

❦

A PROMISE FROM PROVERBS 2:2-6 reveals how to pray for wisdom. "Incline your ear to wisdom, and apply your heart to understanding; yes, if you cry out for discernment, and lift up your voice for understanding, if you seek her as silver, and search for her as for hidden treasures; then you will understand the fear of the LORD, and find the knowledge of God. For the LORD gives wisdom; from His mouth come knowledge and understanding."

Immortal, invisible, God only wise, in light inaccessible hid from my eyes, I confess my lack of wisdom to solve the problems I'm facing. The best of my education, experience, and erudition is not enough. I turn to You and ask for the gift of wisdom. You never tire of offering it, I desire it, and these times require it.

I am stunned by the qualifications of receiving wisdom. Proverbs reminds me that the secret is creative fear of You. What does it mean to fear You? You have taught me that it is really awe, wonder, and humble adoration. My profound concern is that I might be satisfied with my surface analysis and be unresponsive to Your offer of wisdom. Lord, grant me the knowledge and understanding of Your wisdom so that I may speak Your words on my lips. When nothing less will do, You give wisdom to those who humbly ask for it. Thank You, God. Amen.

I thank You and praise You, O God of my fathers;
You have given me wisdom and might.

DANIEL 2:23

Do not be wise in your own opinion.

ROMANS 12:16

If any of you lacks wisdom, let him ask of God, who gives to
all liberally and without reproach and it will be given to him.

JAMES 1:5

The wisdom of God that is from above is first pure,
then peaceable, gentle, willing to yield, full of mercy and
good fruits, without partiality and without hypocrisy.

JAMES 3:17

Knowledge is horizontal. Wisdom is vertical—it
comes down from above.

—⌒ *Billy Graham* ⌒—

When I Long to Make a Difference

❧❧❧

$\mathcal{L}$OVING FATHER, YOU KNOW ME as I really am. You see beneath the surface of my projected adequacy. You know my true needs. The great need, at the core of all my needs, is to truly experience Your presence. I need You, dear God. You delight in me when I desire You above all else. More than anything You can give me or do for me, I long to live in vital communication with You. In this moment of honest prayer, I turn over to You the longings of my heart: everything from my most personal anxieties to my relationships and responsibilities. How wonderful it is to know that You have motivated me to pray because You have solutions and resolutions for my most complex problems!

Lord God of truth, I praise You for the revelation of Your truth to people through history. I thank You for the lodestar leadership of Nathan Hale, the courageous revolutionary patriot, who in the moments before he was hung said, "I only regret that I have but one life to lose for my country." His grandson, Everett Hale, Chaplain of the Senate from 1903 to 1909, gave me another memorable saying that becomes the theme of my prayerful reflection: "I am only one, but I am one. I cannot do everything, but I can do something. What I can do, I should do and, with the help of God, I will do!"

Father, thank You that You have a plan for me. Give me Everett Hale's determination to trust You for the power to follow through on what You have given me the clear conviction to do. Bless me with incisive intentionality for the challenges of this day. You are my Lord and Saviour. Amen.

The program of God through history is like a relay race. Let one runner drop out and the whole team loses. Let one runner lose the baton and the whole team is eliminated. Let one runner break the rules and the whole team is disqualified. The work of no runner counts until every runner does his share and the anchor man has hit the tape at the finish line.

The phrase "let us keep our eyes fixed on Jesus" is the key. The idea is clear. There are lots of distractions as we run. Bypaths beckon us; false goals attract us; competition discourages us; opposition causes us to falter. Jesus, however, a tried and trusted leader who blazed the trail of faith by His own obedience and perseverance and who finished the course in a burst of glory, is both our guide and our goal. We look away from everything else to Him, if we want to run well.*

—◦ David Hubbard ◦—

---

* David Hubbard, *Is Life Really Worth Living?* (Ventura, CA: Gospel Light Publications, 1974); quoted in Fred Bock, comp., *Hymns for the Family of God* (Nashville, TN: Paragon Assoc., 1976), p. 615.

PART V

IN TIMES
OF TRYING
RELATIONSHIPS

When I Need to Communicate Love

Love is patient, love is kind and is not jealous; love does not brag and is not arrogant, does not act unbecomingly; it does not seek its own, is not provoked, does not take into account a wrong suffered, does not rejoice in unrighteousness, but rejoices with the truth; bears all things, believes all things, hopes all things, endures all things.

1 CORINTHIANS 13:4-7 NASB

℮℮℮

O GOD OF LOVE, GIVE ME A FRESH experience of Your love today. Help me to think about how much You love me with unqualified acceptance and forgiveness. May the tone and tenor of my words to the people in my life be an expression of Your love. You have called me to love as You have loved me. May I know when to express not only Your tough love but also when to be tender in withholding judgment or condemnation. Help me to love those I find it difficult to bear and those who find it a challenge to bear with me.

All around me are people with highly polished exteriors that hide their real need for esteem, affirmation, and encouragement from me. Show me practical ways to express love in creative ways. May I lift burdens rather than become one; may I add to people's strength rather than being a source of stress. Place on my agendas the particular people to whom You have called me to communicate Your love. And give me that resolve of which great days are made: If no one else does, Lord, I will!

Place in my mind loving thoughts and feelings for the people in my life. Show me caring things I can do to enact what's in my heart. Direct specific acts of caring You have motivated in my heart. Don't let me forget, Lord. Give me the will to act, to say what I feel. Through Him who is Your amazing Grace. Amen.

1. I will begin each day with an unreserved commitment of my life to Christ.

2. I will invite Christ to fill me with His Spirit: my mind to think His thoughts, my emotions to express His love, and my will to discern and do His will.

3. I will focus on the specific opportunities and challenges in my relationships and responsibilities in the day ahead, and will surrender each of these to Christ and ask for supernatural power, wisdom, and guidance.

4. I promise to pray for people on my heart by name, picturing them and asking for Christ's special empowering. During the day, as they are brought to my mind or I learn of special needs, I will accept these as nudges to intercede for them.

5. I will end the day with a time of reflection on how the Lord blessed and empowered me and others so that gratitude and praise will conclude each day.

When Life Becomes a Tangled
Ball of Misunderstandings

Almighty God, take charge of my thinking brain. Think Your thoughts through me. Give me a mind responsive to Your guidance.

Take charge of my tongue so it may speak truth with clarity, without rancor or anger. May my words be an effort to reach an agreement rather than simply to win arguments. Help me to think of others as fellow strugglers seeking Your best for their own tough times, rather than enemies seeking to defeat me. Make me a channel of Your grace to others. May I respond to Your nudges to communicate affirmation and encouragement.

Help me to catch the drumbeat of your direction and march to the cadence of your guidance. Here is my life. Inspire it with Your calming Spirit, strengthen it with Your powerful presence, and imbue it with Your gift of faith to trust You to unravel the tangled ball of misunderstandings and miscommunications that seem to be part of living today. Help me untie the knots and straighten out the snags.

Lord, I have to admit to You that sometimes it is very difficult to be the initiator and be the first to seek resolution and reconciliation. I get caught up in how right I am rather than being the one who breaks the cycle of recrimination and retaliation. Then I think of Your prevenient grace. You are always beforehand; You make the first move toward me and help me respond. I commit this day to be the one who makes the first move toward others with whom I am estranged. Help me, Lord! Amen.

How the Lord Can Use Misunderstandings

Jesus Christ has made us an awesome promise for those times when we're misunderstood. It was first given to His followers as the assurance of His power when they would be put on trial because of their faith in Him. The promise is equally applicable for our conversations or communicating our faith. It is crucial for anyone who wants to talk in a way that will be understood.

After Jesus had explained that His followers would be brought before the synagogues, kings, and rulers for His sake, He made this promise, "It will turn out for you as an occasion for testimony. Therefore settle it in your hearts not to meditate beforehand on what you will answer; for I will give you a mouth and wisdom which all your adversaries will not be able to contradict or resist" (Luke 21:13-15).

When misunderstandings occur, we can claim that the Lord will use them for what He called "an occasion for testimony." For us today, that means that He will help us handle misunderstandings in a way that shows others His grace at work in us. Because of His love for us, we are freed from either self-pity or blaming others when misunderstandings occur. We can readily admit what we might have done to cause a breakdown of communication, and express our desire to really listen to people.

We don't always have to be right or win every argument. Our openness and flexibility will impress people and may give us an opportunity to share our faith with them. Since feeling misunderstood is such a distressing problem for most people, causing grief and unhappiness, showing them Christ's method of dealing with conflict will be a powerful witness.

When People I Love Are in Trouble Because of Separation from God

❧❧❧

DEAR GOD, YOU HAVE CALLED ME to the awesome opportunity of intercessory prayer. Today, I want to pray for the people You have put on my prayer agenda who are in trouble because of sin in their lives. I know from my own life the pain and anguish my own sins have caused me and other people. Out of gratitude and praise for Your forgiveness of me, I want to pray for people I love. Lord, before it's too late, open their hearts to Your love. Now in this time of intimate conversation with You, show me how I can be part of Your pursuit of them. Enable me to know what to do and say, when and how I am to incarnate Your love by intervening with comfort or confrontation.

Dear God, thank You for not tolerating the sin of the world. Because You cared, You came in Jesus Christ to reconcile us to Yourself. You did not tolerate my rebellion, but invaded me with love and forgiveness. Give me the courage to do more than tolerate people. Help me to remember what life was like before I knew You personally. May that shock me out of bland aloofness from the peril in which people around me are living. Thank You for giving me joy and hope to share. Clarify for me the people in my life who have been prepared by You for a loving and decisive confrontation.

Gracious God, You also have shown me what authentic graciousness is. I want to live this day as a gracious person. You have made me a host for the strangers of the world. I commit the hours of this day to hospitality. Flow through my words and actions as I meet people who are strangers because of their estrangement from You. I offer an open heart to welcome them in Your name. Amen.

PRAYER

More things are wrought by prayer
Than this world dreams of. Wherefore, let thy voice
Rise like a fountain for me night and day.
For what are men better than sheep or goats
That nourish a blind life within the brain,
If, knowing God, they lift not hands of prayer
Both for themselves and those who call them friend?
For so the whole round earth is every way
Bound by gold chains about the feet of God.

Alfred, Lord Tennyson
from "Idylls of the King"

When Judgments Divide

❧∞❧

ALMIGHTY GOD, YOU HAVE CREATED ME in Your own image; forgive me when I return the compliment by trying to create You in my image, projecting onto You my human judgmentalism. I evade Your judgment of my judgments. My judgments divide me from others. I condemn those who differ with me; I miss Your lordship by lording it over others.

I need to be reconciled to You, Lord. Forgive any pride, prejudice, and presumption. People are deeply wounded by cutting words and hurting attitudes toward their religions, races, and political parties. Life is divided into camps of liberal and conservative, this party or that party, and from each camp we shout demeaning criticism of each other.

Forgive my arrogance, but also forgive my reluctance to work together with those with whom I differ. I confess that Your work is held back because of intolerance. I also know that You are the instigator of my longing to be one with You and the inspiration of oneness. Bind me together with others with the triple-braided cord of Your acceptance, atonement, and affirmation.

God of peace, I seek to receive Your peace and communicate it to others throughout this day. I confess anything that may be disturbing my inner peace. I know that if I want peace in my heart, I cannot harbor resentment. I seek forgiveness for any negative criticism, gossip, or innuendo I may have spoken. Forgive the times I have brought acrimony into my relationships instead of bringing peace into misunderstandings. You have shown me that being a reconciler is essential for a continued, sustained experience of Your peace. Most of all, I know that lasting peace results from Your indwelling Spirit, Your presence in my mind and heart.

Show me how to become a communicator of the peace that passes understanding, bringing healing reconciliation, deeper understanding, and open communication. In the name of the Prince of peace, even Jesus Christ our Lord. Amen.

Judge not, that you be not judged.
For with the judgment you judge, you will be judged.

MATTHEW 7:1-2

Let us not judge one another anymore.

ROMANS 14:13

Who are you to judge another?

JAMES 4:12

He Himself is our peace, who has made both one,
and has broken down the middle wall of separation,
having abolished in His flesh the enmity, that is, the law of
commandments contained in ordinances, so as to create
in Himself one new man from the two, thus making peace,
and that He might reconcile them both to God in one body
through the cross, thereby putting to death the enmity.

EPHESIANS 2:14-16

A man's judgment of another depends more on the
one judging and on his passions than on the one
being judged and on his conduct.

 Paul Tournier

When I Need Reconciliation

ALMIGHTY GOD, I CONFESS ANYTHING that stands between me and You and between me and anyone else. I long to be in a right relationship with You again. I know the love, joy, and peace that flood my being when I am reconciled with You. I become a riverbed for the flow of Your supernatural gifts of leadership: wisdom, knowledge, discernment, vision, and authentic charisma.

I confess the pride that estranges me from You and the judgmentalism that strains my relationships. Forgive my cutting words and hurting attitudes toward other religions or races and people with different beliefs, political preferences, or convictions on issues. So often people are divided into camps and opposing groups and I am critical of those with whom I disagree. Help me to express to others the grace I have received in being reconciled to You.

May my efforts to reach out to others be a way of telling You how much I love You. You are my Lord and Saviour. In the Name of Christ who gave me the eleventh commandment, His own: "A new commandment I give to you, that you love one another; as I have loved you, that you also love one another" (John 13:34). Amen.

The Message of Reconciliation

If anyone is in Christ, he is a new creation;
old things have passed away; behold, all things have become
new. Now all things are of God, who has reconciled us to
Himself through Jesus Christ, and has given us the ministry
of reconciliation, that is, that God was in Christ reconciling
the world to Himself, not imputing their trespasses to them,
and has committed to us the word of reconciliation.

Now then, we are ambassadors for Christ, as though God
were pleading through us: we implore you on Christ's behalf,
be reconciled to God. For He made Him who knew
no sin to be sin for us, that we might become
the righteousness of God in Him.

2 CORINTHIANS 5:17-21

When Walls Separate Me

❦

GOD OF PEACE, I CONFESS THE WALLS I build around my own soul, between me and others and between me and You. So often I hold You at arm's length, usually when I need You the most. It's hard for me to confess my dependence on Your wisdom and strength. Then my lack of trust in You impacts my relationships. Forgetting that each person is a unique, never-to-be-repeated miracle of Your grace, I get distracted with competition, comparisons, or power struggles. Added to this, I get obsessed with titles and turf, positions and protocol. Sometimes my political loyalties keep me from affirming my greater loyalty to You and to our nation. Grant me the greatness of seeking to make others great.

Dear Father, help me to extend to others the grace You have extended to me. Grant me freedom from resentments over hurts in the past, and from double standards that require more of others than of myself.

Help me to hear Your call and perceive Your purpose for me above all the other voices that clamor for attention in my life. Deliver me, I pray, from a bland and drifting life. Enable me to focus on what I should do, and to do that on which I focus. In Jesus' dear name I pray. Amen.

Bear one another's burdens, and so fulfill the law of Christ.
GALATIANS 6:2

The Spirit…helps in our weaknesses. For we do not know what we should pray for as we ought, but the Spirit Himself makes intercession for us with groanings which cannot be uttered. Now He who searches the heart knows what the mind of the Spirit is, because He makes intercession for the saints according to the will of God.
ROMANS 8:26-27

[I] do not cease to pray for you.
COLOSSIANS 1:9

I thank my God upon every remembrance of you, always in every prayer of mine making request for you all with joy.
PHILIPPIANS 1:3-4

God is my witness, whom I serve with my spirit in the gospel of His Son, that without ceasing I make mention of you always in my prayers.
ROMANS 1:9

When I Need to Be Sensitive to the Needs of Others

❧❧❧

Loving God, You have blessed me so that I may be a vital part of Your blessing to others. I commit myself to be sensitive to the needs of others around me. Show me the people who particularly need encouragement or affirmation. Give me exactly what I should say to uplift them. Free me of preoccupation with myself and my own needs. Help me to remember that people will care about *what* I know when they know I care about them. May my countenance, words, and actions communicate my caring. Make me a good listener and enable me to hear what people are expressing beneath what they are saying.

Most of all, remind me of the power of intercessory prayer. May I claim Your best for people as I pray for them. Especially I pray for those with whom I disagree on issues. Help me to see them not as enemies but as people who will help sharpen my edge. Lift me above petty attitudes or petulant gossip. Fill this day with Your presence, and my heart with Your magnanimous attitude toward others.

Enlarge my heart until it is big enough to contain the gift of Your Spirit; expand my mind until I am capable of thinking Your thoughts; deepen my trust so I can live with freedom from anxiety. I commit my life into Your capable hands. Amen.

You have heard that it was said, "You shall love your neighbor and hate your enemy." But I say to you, love your enemies, bless those who curse you, do good to those who hate you, and pray for those who spitefully use you and persecute you, that you may be sons of your Father in heaven; for He makes His sun rise on the evil and on the good, and sends rain on the just and on the unjust. For if you love those who love you, what reward have you? Do not even the tax collectors do the same? And if you greet your brethren only, what do you do more than others? Do not even the tax collectors do so? Therefore you shall be perfect, just as your Father in heaven is perfect.

MATTHEW 5:43-48

A new commandment I give to you, that you love one another; as I have loved you, that you also love one another. By this all will know that you are My disciples, if you have love for one another.

JOHN 13:34-35

When they had eaten breakfast, Jesus said to Simon Peter, "Simon, son of Jonah, do you love Me more than these?" He said to Him, "Yes, Lord; You know that I love You." He said to him, "Feed My lambs." He said to him again a second time, "Simon, son of Jonah, do you love Me?" He said to Him, "Yes, Lord; you know that I love You." He said to him, "Tend My sheep." He said to him the third time, "Simon, son of Jonah, do you love Me?" Peter was grieved because He said to him the third time, "Do you love Me?" And he said to Him, "Lord, You know all things; You know that I love You." Jesus said to him, "Feed my sheep."

JOHN 21:15-17

When I Need to Pray for Others

❦❧

LORD, I ASK YOU FOR A VERY SPECIAL GIFT. This gift is one I know You want to give. It is for the awareness of the power of prayer for others. You have told me in the Scriptures that there are blessings You grant only when I care enough to pray for people. I also know how my attitude is changed when I pray for loved ones and friends. I listen better, and conflicts are resolved. I discover answers to problems together with them because prayer has made it easier to work out solutions.

Also, when I pray for others, You affirm my caring by releasing supernatural power. Working together becomes more pleasant and more productive. Knowing this, I make a renewed commitment to pray for the people around me, those with whom I disagree theologically or politically, and those with whom I sometimes find it difficult to work.

Father, I commit myself to be a peacemaker. I confess that it is so easy to sow discord, fan fires of misunderstanding between people, and take sides in conflicts. I ask for the gift of peace so I can experience and express Christ's serenity, tranquility, and reconciliation. Help me be quick to forgive, slow to judge, and resourceful when people are at odds with each other. I want to be a reconciler who brings estranged people and groups together.

I can't produce peace, but I can propagate the peace that already has been given to me through the blood of Christ on the cross. I want every person to possess that kind of peace to heal their broken and strained relationships. I want every compound fracture between groups to be reset by it, all misunderstandings and hatred to be liberated by it. You have told me that the only way to be happy and truly blessed is to become involved in peacemaking. Thank You for offering me a partnership in Your family business. Amen.

Bear one another's burdens,
and so fulfill the law of Christ.
GALATIANS 6:2

As for me, far be it from me that I should sin
against the LORD in ceasing to pray for you.
1 SAMUEL 12:23

This is the confidence that we may have before Him,
that if we ask anything according to His will, He hears us.
And if we know that He hears us whatever we ask, we know
that we have the petitions that we have asked of Him.
1 JOHN 5:14-15

I will give you the keys of the kingdom of heaven,
and whatever you bind on earth will be bound in heaven,
and whatever you loose on earth will be loosed in heaven.
MATTHEW 16:19

Beloved, let us love one another, for love is of God;
and everyone who loves is born of God and knows God.
He who does not love does not know God, for God is love.
In this the love of God was manifested toward us,
that God has sent His only begotten Son into the world,
that we might live through Him.
1 JOHN 4:7-9

When I Need to Have My Lockjaw Healed

GRACIOUS FATHER, THANK YOU for Your blessing. It gives me approbation, affirmation, a feeling of value, a sense of destiny, and an assurance of Your power. You have chosen, cherished, and called me to be Your child. In Your providential planning You have placed me where I am and given me special assignments. You have given unique orders for the work I am to do. You provide power to help me, for You have ordained that if I do not do the work You have given me to do, it will not be done. So I report in for duty with the delight that I have been blessed to be a blessing.

Help me to bless the people of my life with a reminder of how much they mean to me. Heal my lockjaw so I can articulate my appreciation for the gift of each person. May I be used by You to fill the blessing-shaped void inside of everyone needing to be uplifted by words of encouragement.

I will live this day only once. Before it's gone, may I bless all the people I can in every way I can, with all the love I can. Help me not to waste today in selfish neglect of the people You have given me. Today is a day to receive and to give Your blessing.

I thank You for the blessings of my life. Help me to see them, to count them, and to remember them so my life may flow in ceaseless praise. Give me eyes to see the invisible movement of Your Spirit in people and in events. Assure me that You are present, working out Your purposes because You have plans for me. Focus my attention on the amazing way You work through people—arranging details, solving complexities, and bringing good out of whatever difficulties I commit to You. Help me to be expectant of Your serendipities, Your unusual acts of love in usual circumstances. Now I look forward to a great day filled with Your grace! In Your generous, giving, and forgiving name—Jesus Christ, my Lord. Amen.

Fear not, I will help you.

ISAIAH 41:13

Blessed be the LORD,
Because He has heard the voice of my supplications!
The LORD is my strength and my shield;
My heart trusted in Him, and I am helped;
Therefore my heart greatly rejoices,
And with my song I will praise Him.

PSALM 28:6-7

He says, "In an acceptable time I have heard you,
and in the day of salvation I have helped you."

2 CORINTHIANS 6:2

Oh, give thanks to the LORD!
Call upon His name;
Make known His deeds among the peoples!
Sing to Him, sing psalms to Him;
Talk of all His wondrous works!
Glory in His holy name;
Let the hearts of those rejoice who seek the LORD!

PSALM 105:1-3

Seek the LORD and His strength;
Seek His face evermore!
Remember His marvelous works which He has done,
His wonders, and the judgments of His mouth.

PSALM 105:4-5

When I Need to
Make a Fresh Start

❧❧❧

*G*RACIOUS FATHER, GIVER OF EVERY GOOD gift for my growth as Your child, I acknowledge my utter dependence on You. I have nothing I have not received from You. You sustain me day by day, moment by moment. I deliberately empty my mind and heart of anything that does not glorify You. I release to You any pride, self-serving attitude, or willfulness I may have harbored in my heart. I ask You to take from me anything that makes it difficult not only to love, but to like, certain people. May my relationships reflect Your initiative, love, and forgiveness.

Dear God, so often in my prayers I present You with my own agenda. I ask for guidance and strength and courage to do what I have already decided. Usually, what I have in mind is to receive from You what I think I need in order to get on with my prearranged plans. Often I present my shopping list of the blessings I have in mind for my projects, many of which I may not have checked out with You in the first place. Sometimes I make little time to talk to You or listen to You.

Any blessing I receive is empty unless I also receive a deeper fellowship with You. Help me to think of prayer throughout this day as simply reporting in for duty and *asking for fresh marching orders*. I want to be all that You want me to be, and I want to do what You have planned for me. May this prayer be the beginning of a conversation with You that lasts all through the day. Help me to attempt something I could not do without Your power. In the name of Christ who calls me to admit my need, submit my failures, and commit my life to make a fresh start. Amen.

Recapitulation, Resurrection, Regeneration:
Three momentous words;
Words of great hope.
Christ's death and resurrection are
recapitulated in us when we surrender
our lives to Him.
We die to self-sovereignty; we are born again.
A new person is raised up in us,
We are a new creature.
A new creation.
Old things pass away, the new has come.
We are ready to be filled with the Holy Spirit.
Our regeneration begins.
Each day we are filled afresh.
Our transformation continues.
We have been called, chosen, destined
to be made like Christ.
Fear of death is gone;
All our physical death can do to us
is to release us to a fuller realization of heaven
we have begun to experience now.

—*Lloyd John Ogilvie*—

When My Motives
Need Mending

⁓⊗⊱⊗⁓

$\mathcal{A}$LMIGHTY GOD, ULTIMATE JUDGE of my life, in this moment of quiet reflection, I hold up my motives for Your review. I want to be totally honest with You and with myself about what really motivates my decisions, words, and actions. Sometimes I want You to approve of motives I have not even reviewed in light of Your righteousness, justice, and love. There are times when I am driven by self-serving motives that contradict my better nature.

Most serious of all, I confess that sometimes my motives are dominated by secondary loyalties: ambition blurs my vision; combative competition prompts manipulative methods; negative attitudes foster strained relationships. I ask You to purify my motives and refine them until they are in congruity with Your will and Your vision for my life. When I put You first in my life, You bring results I could not achieve by human methods alone. I thank You in advance for performing these miracles.

Sovereign God, You are my help in all the ups and downs of life, all the triumphs and defeats, and all the changes and challenges. You are my Lord in all seasons and for all reasons. I can come to You when life makes me glad or sad. There is no circumstance beyond Your control. Wherever I go, You are there waiting for me. You are already at work with people before I encounter them. You prepare solutions for my complexities, and You are always ready to help me resolve conflicts even before I ask.

My only goal is to please You in what I say and accomplish. Give me Your strength to endure and Your courage to triumph in things great and small that I attempt for the good of all. In Christ's name. Amen.

O Lord, You have searched me and known me.
You know my sitting down and my rising up;
You understand my thought afar off.
You comprehend my path and my lying down,
And are acquainted with all my ways.
For there is not a word on my tongue,
But behold, O Lord, You know it altogether.
You have hedged me behind and before,
And laid Your hand upon me.
Such knowledge is too wonderful for me;
It is high, I cannot attain it.

Where can I go from Your Spirit?
Or where can I flee from Your presence?
If I ascend into heaven, You are there;
If I make my bed in hell, behold, You are there.
If I take the wings of the morning,
And dwell in the uttermost parts of the sea,
Even there Your hand shall lead me,
And Your right hand shall hold me.
If I say, "Surely the darkness shall fall on me,"
Even the night shall be light about me;
Indeed, the darkness shall not hide from You,
But the night shines as the day;
The darkness and the light are both alike to You...

Search me, O God, and know my heart;
Try me, and know my anxieties;
And see if there is any wicked way in me,
And lead me in the way everlasting.

PSALM 139:1-12,23-24

When Responsibilities
Are Heavy

I will hope continually,
And will praise you yet more and more.
My mouth shall tell of Your righteousness
And Your salvation all the day,
For I do not know their limits.
I will go in the strength of the Lord GOD;
I will make mention of Your righteousness, of Yours only.

PSALM 71:14-16

⸜⸝

ALMIGHTY GOD, A TIME OF HEAVY responsibilities stretches out before me. As I face these responsibilities, I thank You for Winston Churchill's reminder that "the price of greatness is responsibility." Father, You have entrusted me with awesome challenges. Thank You that You will not ask more from me than You will give the strength to carry. Help me to draw on Your artesian wells of wisdom, insight, discernment, and vision. Be with me in the lonely hours of decision-making, of conflict over issues, and the ruthless demands of an overloaded schedule. Tenderly whisper in my soul the reassurance, "I have placed you here and will not leave you, nor forsake you."

In Your grace, be with my loved ones. Watch over them and reassure me that You care for the loved ones of those who assume heavy responsibilities for You. May responsibility come to mean "respondability," a response of trust in You to carry out what You have entrusted to me. In the name of Christ who lifts burdens and carries the load. Amen.

Your ears shall hear a word behind you saying,
"This is the way, walk in it."

ISAIAH 30:21

Hear my prayer, O LORD, give ear to my supplications!
In Your faithfulness answer me, and in Your righteousness.

PSALM 143:1

You are the salt of the earth; but if the salt loses its flavor,
how shall it be seasoned? It is then good for nothing
but to be thrown out and trampled underfoot by men.
You are the light of the world. A city that is set on
a hill cannot be hidden. Nor do they light a lamp and
put it under a basket, but on a lampstand,
and it gives light to all who are in the house. Let your
light so shine before men, that they may see your
good works and glorify Your Father in heaven.

MATTHEW 5:13-16

In the pure, strong hours of the morning when the
soul of the day is at its best, lean upon the windowsill
of God and look into His face, and get the orders for
the day. Then go out into the day with the sense of a
Hand upon your shoulder and not a chip.

E. Stanley Jones

When I Long for
Renewed Purpose

❧❧❧

THE PSALMIST DRAWS MY HEART and mind to You, dear God: "O LORD, our Lord, how excellent is Your name in all the earth...What is man that You are mindful of him, and the son of man that You visit him? For You have made him a little lower than the angels, and You have crowned him with glory and honor. You have made him to have dominion over the works of your hands" (Psalm 8:1,4-6).

Gracious God, ultimate Sovereign and Lord of my life, I am stunned again by Your majesty and the magnitude of the delegated dominion You have entrusted to me. I respond with awe and wonder and with renewed commitment to be a servant leader. In a culture that often denies Your sovereignty and worships at the throne of the perpendicular pronoun—"I"—help me to exemplify the greatness of servanthood. You have given me a life full of opportunities to serve, freed me more and more from self-serving aggrandizement, and enabled me to live at full potential for Your glory. I humble myself before You and acknowledge that I could not breathe a breath, think a thought, make a decision, or press on to excellence without Your power. By Your appointment I am where I am doing the work You have given me to do: called to serve others. You alone are the one I seek to please. I have been blessed to be a blessing. Grant me grace and courage to give myself away to You and to others with whom I am privileged to live and work today. Amen.

For to me, to live is Christ.

PHILIPPIANS 1:21

Indeed I also count all things loss for the excellence of
the knowledge of Christ Jesus my Lord, for whom I have
suffered the loss of all things, and count them as rubbish,
that I may gain Christ and be found in Him, not having my
own righteousness, which is from the law, but that which is
through faith in Christ, the righteousness which is from
God by faith; that I may know Him and the power of His
resurrection, and the fellowship of His sufferings, being conformed to His death, if, by any means, I may attain to the
resurrection from the dead.

Not that I have already attained, or am already perfected;
but I press on, that I may lay hold of that for which Christ
Jesus has also laid hold of me. Brethren, I do not count
myself to have apprehended; but one thing I do, forgetting
those things which are behind and reaching forward to those
things which are ahead, I press toward the goal for the prize
of the upward call of God in Christ Jesus.

PHILIPPIANS 3:8-14

I have fought the good fight, I have finished the race,
I have kept the faith.

2 TIMOTHY 4:7

Man, made in the image of God, has a purpose—to
be in relationship to God who is there. Man forgets
his purpose and thus he forgets who he is and what
life means.

—⁖ *Francis A. Schaeffer* ⁖—

PRAYING THROUGH THE TOUGH TIMES

When Praise
Is the Answer

❧❦❧

BLESSED GOD, OUR FATHER, You have shown me that there is great spiritual power in praise. When I praise You, my mind and heart are opened to Your Spirit, burdens are lifted, problems are resolved, and strength is released. So I join my voice with the psalmist: "I will tell of all Your marvelous works. I will be glad and rejoice in You; I will sing praise to Your name, O Most High" (Psalm 9:1-2).

I confess that often it is difficult to praise You in troublesome times and with frustrating people. And yet, it is when I deliberately praise You for them that I receive fresh inspiration. Help me remember what You have taught me: Praising You for the most challenging situations and contentious people transforms me and my attitudes, as well as them.

Give me greater confidence in Your inner working in people and in Your unseen but powerful presence in every situation. Again I join the psalmist, "Because Your lovingkindness is better than life, my lips shall praise You. Thus I will bless You while I live" (Psalm 63:3-4). This is a day to praise You, O Lord! Amen.

Oh, give thanks to the LORD!
Call upon His name;
Make known His deeds among the peoples!
Sing to Him, sing psalms to Him;
Talk of all His wondrous works!
Glory in His holy name;
Let the hearts of those rejoice who seek the LORD!
Seek the LORD and His strength;
Seek His face evermore!
Remember His marvelous works which He has done,
His wonders and the judgments of His mouth,
O seed of Israel His servant,
You children of Jacob, His chosen ones!

He is the LORD our God;
His judgments are in all the earth.
Remember His covenant forever,
The word which He commanded, for a thousand
generations,
The covenant which He made with Abraham,
And His oath to Isaac,
And confirmed it to Jacob for a statute.

1 CHRONICLES 16:8-17

Sing to the LORD, all the earth;
Proclaim the good news of His salvation from day to day.
Declare His glory among the nations,
His wonders among all peoples.
For the LORD is great and greatly to be praised.

1 CHRONICLES 16:23-25

❧

PART VI

In Times of Concern over World Unrest

When I Panic over Terrorism

❧❧❧

ALMIGHTY GOD, SOURCE OF STRENGTH and hope in the darkest hours of our nation's history, I praise You for the consistency and constancy of Your presence to help me and my fellow citizens to confront and battle the forces of evil manifested in infamous, elusive, cowardly acts of terrorism. My heart still is filled with dismay, anger, and grief over the terrorist attacks on September 11, 2001, on the World Trade Center in New York, on the Pentagon in Washington, and on the victims of that fourth plane that crashed before reaching the Capitol. I remember with grief and gratitude the heroes and heroines aboard that plane who forced it down, sacrificing their own lives, but saving thousands of others.

So often my mind focuses on the families of those gallant Americans and the thousands of victims who lost their lives on that infamous day. Like so many, I feel panic about the future living in a world tormented by terrorist groups and movements. Hardly a day goes by without some new catastrophe.

I ask that You quiet my turbulent heart. As I am reminded of the dangerous days in which I am living, also remind me that You are in control. You have been with this nation in trouble and tragedies of the past and have given us victory over tyranny.

I put my trust in You. I belong to You now and for eternity. I need not panic. Instead I pray for Your protection for America and a rebirth of patriotism as I support the President, Congress, and the men and women of the armed forces. God, bless America! Amen.

God is our refuge and strength,
A very present help in trouble.
Therefore we will not fear,
Even though the earth be removed,
And though the mountains be carried
into the midst of the sea;
Though its waters roar and be troubled,
Though the mountains shake with its swelling. *Selah.*

There is a river whose streams shall
make glad the city of God,
The holy place of the tabernacle of the Most High.
God is in the midst of her, she shall not be moved;
God shall help her, just at the break of dawn.
The nations raged, the kingdoms were moved;
He uttered His voice, the earth melted.

The Lord of hosts is with us;
The God of Jacob is our refuge. *Selah.*

Come, behold the works of the Lord,
Who has made desolations in the earth.
He makes wars cease to the end of the earth;
He breaks the bow and cuts the spear in two;
He burns the chariot in the fire.

Be still, and know that I am God;
I will be exalted among the nations,
I will be exalted in the earth!

The Lord of hosts is with us,
The God of Jacob is our refuge. *Selah.*

PSALM 46

When I Am Troubled

❧❧❧

*G*RACIOUS GOD, A VERY PRESENT HELP in trouble, I praise You for giving me Your tenacity to live through troubled times. I listen in on Your conversation with the psalmist when he was beset with trouble. I hear Your gracious invitation: "Call on Me in the day of trouble; I will deliver you, and you shall glorify Me" (Psalm 50:15). I respond with the psalmist, "Hear my prayer, O LORD. Do not hide Your face from me in the day of my trouble; incline Your ear to me…Though I walk in the midst of trouble, You will revive me" (Psalm 102:1; 138:7).

Thank You, Lord, for Your reviving power. You revive me with convictions that cannot be compromised: You are my refuge and our strength; You have blessed our nation through our history; You will help us be victorious over the evil of those who wish us harm. I am revived also by the replenishing of my confidence: You will save me through my present crisis; I need not fear. I feel Your Spirit surging into my soul: anxiety is replaced by serene security, frustration by faith, tiredness with tenacity, and caution with courage. And so I say with the psalmist, "In the day when I cried out, You answered me, and made me bold with strength in my soul" (Psalm 138:3). Amen.

Passing Through

"When Thou passest through the waters,"
Deep the waves may be, and cold,
But Jehovah is our refuge
And His promise is our hold;
For the Lord Himself hath said it,
He the faithful God and true;
When thou comest to the waters,
Thou shalt *not go down,* but *through.*

Seas of sorrow, seas of trial,
Bitterest anguish, fiercest pain,
Rolling surges of temptation,
Sweeping over heart and brain,
They shall never overflow us,
For we know His word is true;
All His waves and all His billows
He will *lead us safely through.*

Threatening breakers of destruction,
Doubt's insidious undertow,
Shall not sink us, shall not drag us
Out to ocean depths of woe;
For His promise shall sustain us,
Praise the Lord, whose word is true!
We shall not go down or under,
He hath said, "Thou passest *through.*"

— *Annie Johnson Flint*

When I Need Confidence in God's Control

❧❧❧

ALMIGHTY GOD, IN THESE UNCERTAIN DAYS of future jitters, I want to reaffirm some very powerful presuppositions about You and Your providential care for Your creation. Strengthen my conviction that You do not cause tragedies. I dismiss that false question, "Where was God in the midst of the disaster?" You were with us giving us courage and hope.

You created humankind—to know, to love, and to serve You. I reverently reflect on what must have been Your most crucial decision when You created humankind: You gave us freedom of choice, knowing that there can be no response of love without choice, but also that humankind would abuse this freedom. There is an objective force of evil in the world that often has been expressed through people, and movements, and nations. Heinous acts happen.

You are not dissuaded. You suffer with me and, with ways I could not plan, bring good out of evil. Not even death can separate me from You. This life is but a small part of the whole of eternity. In the midst of my anguish over those who die in tragedies, remind me of the shortness of time and the length of eternity. Make me a communicator of love and strength to those who continue to suffer in the grim outbursts of evil deeds. Bless all of us with a fresh gift of faith to trust You, and a renewed assurance that "though the wrong seems oft so strong, You are the ruler yet!" Amen.

Call upon Me in the day of trouble;
I will deliver you, and you shall glorify Me.

PSALM 50:15

The salvation of the righteous is from the LORD;
He is their strength in the time of trouble.

PSALM 37:39

You are great, and do wondrous things;
You alone are God.

PSALM 86:10

Though I walk in the midst of trouble, You will revive me.

PSALM 138:7

Blessed be the God and Father of our Lord Jesus Christ, the
Father of mercies and God of all comfort, who comforts us
in all our tribulation, that we may be able to comfort those
who are in any trouble, with the comfort with which we
ourselves are comforted by God.

2 CORINTHIANS 1:3-4

When Bad Things Happen

❧❧❧

$\mathcal{L}$ORD, WHEN THINGS GO BAD, I urgently need a fresh experience of Your goodness. You are always consistent, never changing, constantly fulfilling Your plans and purposes, and totally reliable. There is no shadow of turning with You; as You have been, You will be forever. All Your attributes are summed up in Your goodness. It is the password for Your presence, the metonym for Your majesty, and the synonym for Your strength. Your goodness is the generosity that You define. It is Your outrushing, unqualified love poured out in graciousness and compassion. You are good when circumstances seem bad. When I ask for Your help, Your goodness can bring what is best out of the most complicated problems.

Dear God, Your mercies are indefatigable, and Your presence sustains me through the day. I seek to glorify You in all I do and say. You provide me strength for this day, guidance in my decisions, vision for the way, courage in adversity, help from above, unfailing empathy, and unlimited love. You never leave me nor forsake me, nor do You ask of me more than You will provide the resources to accomplish.

Thank You for Your goodness given so lavishly to me in the past. Today, again I turn to You for Your guidance for what is good for me, my family, and my friends. Keep me grounded in Your sovereignty, rooted in Your commandments, and nurtured by the absolutes of Your truth and righteousness. May Your goodness always be the source of the graciousness I long to be able to express today. In the good name of Jesus, my Lord and Saviour. Amen.

I would have lost heart, unless
I had believed that I would see the goodness
of the LORD in the land of the living.

PSALM 27:13

Oh, how great is Your goodness, which You have
laid up for those who fear You [awe and wonder], which You
have prepared for those who trust You in the presence
of the sons of men! You shall hide them in the secret place of
Your presence from the plots of man; You shall keep them
secretly in a pavilion from the strife of tongues.

PSALM 31:19-20

Why do you boast in evil, O mighty man?
The goodness of God endures continually.

PSALM 52:1

Every good gift and every perfect gift is from above,
and comes down from the Father of lights,
with whom there is no variation or shadow of turning.

JAMES 1:17

We know that all that happens to us is working for
our good if we love God and are fitting into His plans.

ROMANS 8:28 TLB

Good news is love in action.

—⌒ *James Hamilton* ⌒—

The Lord's goodness surrounds us every moment.

—⌒ *R.W. Barbour* ⌒—

When Fears Distress Me

❦❧

*L*OVING FATHER, YOU HAVE TOLD ME that Your perfect love casts out fear. I open my mind to think about how much You love me, and open my heart to be filled with Your unlimited love. Remind me that nothing happens without Your permission and that You are able to use everything that happens to me to bring me closer to You.

Therefore, I commit to You the anxieties in my personal and professional life that cause fear of the future. So that I may work today with freedom from fear, I entrust to Your care my loved ones and their needs, my friends who face sickness and problems, my fellow workers who need Your special care. I surrender my fears of the possible failure of my own plans and programs. Thank You for Your bracing assurance through Isaiah, "Fear not, for I am with you; be not dismayed, for I am your God. I will strengthen you, yes, I will help you, I will uphold you with My righteous right hand" (Isaiah 41:10).

Help me to make this a day for optimism and courage. Set me free from any negative thinking or attitude. There is enough time today to accomplish what You have planned. I affirm that I am where I am by Your divine appointment. I also know from experience that it is possible to limit Your best for my life. Without Your help, I can hit wide of the mark, but with Your guidance and power, I cannot fail. I thank You in advance for a truly great day, for You are my Lord and will show the way!

So I press on to the responsibilities of the day with the assurance that Your perfect love will cast out fear all through the day. In the name of Him who never leaves nor forsakes me. Amen.

My fear is really loneliness for God. Therefore, I will claim His promise to never leave or forsake me. I will overcome my crippling fears with a creative fear of God expressed with awe and wonder. I will face my fears, retrace them to their source in my heart, displace them by making my heart Christ's home, and erase them with His perfect love. I will let go of my hurting memories of the past. I will not anticipate the repetition of the past pain; I will accept forgiveness from the Lord and will forgive everything and everyone in the past—including myself.

In response to God's unqualified acceptance, I will embrace myself as worthy of my own affirmation and encouragement. I will conquer my fear by becoming a riverbed for the flow of God's love to others. I will not surrender my self-worth to the opinions and judgments of others. I will allow God to heal me. And knowing the pain of rejection, I will seek to love those who suffer from its anguish.

Today I will turn over the control of my life to the Lord. I confess my fearful imagination, and today I ask the Lord to make my imagination a channel of His vision and not a breeding place of fear. I will face my eventual physical death and claim that I am spiritually alive eternally. Today, I commit myself to motivating people with love rather than manipulating them with fear. I will give up the vague idea that, given time, things work out. I will boldly face the future unafraid, with the sure confidence that God will work all things together for my ultimate good and His glory.

When I Am Tired

⤜⤏⋈⤎⤛

*G*RACIOUS FATHER, IN THESE TROUBLESOME DAYS of conflict and consternation, frustration and fatigue, stress and strain, I come to You seeking Your special tonic for tiredness. I am feeling the energy-sapping tension of this time. I claim Your promise, "As your days, so shall your strength be" (Deuteronomy 33:25). Your strength is perfectly matched for whatever life will dish out today. You promise me the stamina of ever-increasing fortitude. In the quiet of this communion with You, I open the floodgates of my soul and ask You to flood my mind with a refreshing renewal of hope in You, my emotions with a calm confidence in help from You, and my body with invigorating health through You.

I thank You, mighty God, Creator of the universe and Re-creator of those who trust You, for this most crucial appointment of the day with You. You have commanded that I be still and know that You are God. Lift my burdens, show me solutions to my problems, and give me the courage to press on. Through Christ my overcoming Lord. Amen.

I will love You, O Lord, my strength.
The Lord is my rock and my fortress and my deliverer;
My God, my strength, in whom I will trust;
My shield and the horn of my salvation, my stronghold.

PSALM 18:1-2

I will call upon the Lord, who is worthy to be praised.

PSALM 18:3

The hour is coming, and now is, when the true worshipers
will worship the Father in spirit and truth; for the Father
is seeking such to worship Him. God is Spirit, and those
who worship Him must worship in spirit and truth.

JOHN 4:23-24

You are worthy, O Lord,
To receive glory and honor and power;
For You created all things,
And by Your will they exist and were created.

REVELATION 4:11

He has shown you, O man, what is good;
And what does the Lord require of you
But to do justly,
To love mercy,
And to walk humbly with your God?

MICAH 6:8

When Patriotism
Has Not Gone out of Style

❧❧❧

ALMIGHTY GOD, I PRAISE YOU for the religious freedom I enjoy in America. Thank You that the fabric of that freedom was woven by lodestar leaders—like William Penn, who in 1701 published a charter of privileges ensuring that everyone would be given liberty to worship You according to the dictates of his or her beliefs and conscience.

I am moved by the fact that the bell celebrating the jubilee founding of Pennsylvania, cast 50 years later, became the Liberty Bell—which rang during the first reading of the Declaration of Independence in 1776. It is moving to me that an exact replica cast by the same works in England was recently dedicated to be taken around the nation and rung. The words cast into this Spirit of Liberty Bell are the same as the original from Leviticus 25:10: "Proclaim liberty throughout all the land unto all the inhabitants thereof."

As this Spirit of Liberty Bell continues to ring throughout the land, help me to rededicate myself to maintain religious freedom. Forgive any prejudice in my heart, and purge from me any vestige of judgmentalism for people whose expression of faith in You differs from my own. As we battle against evil-doers and nations who persecute people because of their religious beliefs, help me make America a nation where we live by George Washington's motto: "To bigotry, give no sanction…to persecution, no assistance." In Your liberating name. Amen.

God who gave us life, gave us liberty. Can the liberties of a nation be secure when we have removed a conviction that these liberties are a gift of God?

— *Thomas Jefferson* —
inscribed on his memorial, Washington, DC

In 1787, at a pivotal moment at the Constitutional Convention, Benjamin Franklin's convictions led him to rise and speak these now-famous words to George Washington: "I have lived, sir, a long time, and the longer I live the more convincing proofs I see of this truth: that God governs in the affairs of men. If a sparrow cannot fall to the ground without His notice, is it probable that an empire can rise without His aid? I believe that without His concurring aid we shall succeed no better than the builders of Babel. We shall be divided by our partial local interests; our projects will be confounded…"

Lord, it is with the same emphatic certainty that we echo his words of dependence on You—and we ask, Sovereign Lord, that You would help us realize Your best for America.

Our Fathers' God, to Thee,
Author of liberty,
To Thee we sing;
Long may our land be bright
With freedom's holy light;
Protect us by Thy might,
Great God, our King.

— *Reverend Samuel Francis Smith* —

America! America!
God shed His grace on Thee;
And crown thy good with brotherhood
From sea to shining sea!

— *Katherine Lee Bates* —

In response, we open our lives to Your grace and renew our commitment to Your good as the measure of America's greatness. God bless America. Amen.

When I Need to Pray for the Oneness of God and State

❦

ALMIGHTY GOD, SOVEREIGN OF THIS NATION, as You guided our Founding Fathers to establish the separation of church and state to protect the church from the intrusion of government, rather than the intrusion of the church into government, I praise You that in Your providential plan for this nation there is to be no separation of You and state. With gratitude I declare our motto: "In God We Trust." It is with reverence I repeat the words of commitment as part of our Pledge of Allegiance to our flag: "One Nation under God, indivisible."

May these words never become so familiar by repetition that I lose my profound sense of awe and wonder, or my feeling of accountability and responsibility to place my trust in You, seek Your guidance in all decisions, and make patriotism an essential expression of my relationship with You. I praise You for Your truth spelled out in the Bill of Rights and the Constitution. Help me not to take for granted the freedom I enjoy, nor the call You sound in my soul for righteousness in every aspect of this nation. I repent for the moral decay in our culture, any contradiction of Your commandments in our society, and any reluctance to be faithful to You.

Wake me up, and then stir me up with a fresh realization of the unique role You have given this nation to exemplify what it means to be a blessed nation because I and fellow Americans humble ourselves before You and exalt You as our only Sovereign. Lord God of hosts, be with us yet, lest we forget! Amen.

We have no government armed with power capable of contending with human passions unbridled by morality and religion. Avarice, ambition, revenge, or gallantry, would break the strongest cords of our Constitution as a whale goes through a net. Our Constitution was made only for a moral and religious people. It is wholly inadequate to the government of any other.

—◦ *President John Adams, 1798* ◦—

On June 14, 1954, President Dwight Eisenhower signed into law a congressional act that added the phrase "one Nation under God" to the Pledge of Allegiance. Standing on the steps of the Capitol, he said,

> In this way we are reaffirming the transcendence of religious faith in America's heritage and future; in this way we shall constantly strengthen those spiritual weapons which forever will be our country's most powerful resource in peace and war.

On June 14, 2004, the United States Supreme Court ruled to preserve the wording "one Nation under God" in the Pledge of Allegiance.

When I Need to Be Optimistic

The Lord your God in your midst, the Mighty One,
will save; He will rejoice over you with gladness, He will
quiet you with His love, He will rejoice over you with
singing.

Zephaniah 3:17

∞∞∞

Gracious God, give me an assurance of Your unqualified love, profound peace that quiets my heart, and ears tuned to hear Your song of affirmation. I need Your gift of vibrant optimism.

My optimism often is like a tea bag; I never know how strong it is until I get into hot water. In times of frustration or adversity my optimism is tested. When the wheels of organization grind slowly, often I become pessimistic. It is then I need to hear Your song of encouragement. So often I live as if I had to carry the burdens of leadership alone. Today I relinquish to You any negative thoughts, critical attitudes, and impatient moods. Infuse me with Your hope. Again I pray, hope through me today, O God of hope, so that my discouragements will be turned to optimism based on Your faithfulness. "Ring out the bells of the kirk; God is down to Earth to bless those who work!"

Thank You, dear God, that You are closer than my hands and feet and as available for inspiration as my breathing. May this day be lived in companionship with You, so that I will enjoy the confidence of the promise You gave through Isaiah: "It shall come to pass that before they call, I will answer; and while they are still speaking, I will hear" (Isaiah 65:24).

When this day closes, my deepest joy will be that I have worked to achieve Your goals. You are my Lord and Saviour, the Source of true optimism. Amen.

Let us be like a bird for a moment perched on a frail
branch while he sings;
Though he feels it bend, yet he sings his song,
knowing that he has wings.

— Victor Hugo —

The future is as bright as the promises of God.

— Adoniram Judson —

Oh, send out Your light and Your truth!
Let them lead me.

PSALM 43:3

You are my rock and my fortress:
Therefore, for Your name's sake,
Lead me and guide me.

PSALM 31:3

May the road rise up to meet you
May the wind be always at your back,
May the sun lie warm upon your face,
The rain fall softly on your fields
And until we meet again
May the Lord hold you
In the hollow of His hand.

— Gaelic Blessing —

When I Need to
Overcome the Darkness

"Not by might nor by power, but by My Spirit," says the LORD.

ZECHARIAH 4:6

⁂

ALMIGHTY GOD, MY SOVEREIGN LORD, thank You for these salient words reminding me that You are the only reliable source of strength to accomplish anything of lasting value. You remind me that these words spoken through Zechariah and repeated during the days of Hanukkah have particular significance to me in these tough times. I claim the meaning of the word Hanukkah, "dedication," as I rededicate my life to serve You in the struggle to assure religious freedom for all people. I join with Jewish people in the celebration of the Feast of Dedication and remember the victory in 165 B.C. of the Maccabees over the tyrant Antiochus IV Epiphanes and his troops who had occupied Jerusalem, desecrated the temple, and sought to destroy forever the Hebrew religion.

I celebrate this victory that enabled the Jews to rededicate the temple and once again worship You freely. Gratefully, I remember the one remaining flask of pure olive oil left in the temple that You kept burning for eight days and eight nights until the supply could be replenished. Now, when Jews light menorahs, I ask You to light up my heart with Your truth so that I can shine in the spiritual darkness of our time when evil things are done in the name of religion, and where religious freedom is denied so many people. I dedicate myself to battle injustice not by my might or my power, but by the courage of Your Spirit. Amen.

My Help Comes from the Lord

I will lift up my eyes to the hills—from whence comes my
help? My help comes from the Lord,
who made heaven and earth.

He will not allow your foot to be moved; He who keeps you
will not slumber. Behold, He who keeps Israel shall
neither slumber nor sleep.

The Lord is your keeper: the Lord
is your shade at your right hand. The sun shall not strike
you by day, nor the moon by night.

The Lord shall preserve
you from all evil; He shall preserve your soul.
The Lord shall preserve your going out and your coming in
from this time forth, and even forevermore.

Psalm 121

The foolishness of God is wiser than men,
and the weakness of God is stronger than men. For you see
your calling, brethren, that not many wise according to the
flesh, not many mighty, not many noble, are called. But
God has chosen the foolish things of the world to put to
shame the wise, and God has chosen the weak things of the
world to put to shame the things which are mighty; and the
base things of the world and the things which are despised
God has chosen, and the things which are not, to bring to
nothing the things that are, that no flesh should glory in
His presence. But of Him you are in Christ Jesus, who
became for us wisdom from God—and a righteousness and
sanctification and redemption—that, as it is written,
"He who glories, let him glory in the Lord."

1 Corinthians 1:25-31

When I Need a Fresh Touch

❦

ALMIGHTY GOD, IN THESE CHALLENGING DAYS, I remember Abraham Lincoln's words, "I have been driven many times upon my knees by the overwhelming conviction that I had nowhere else to go. My own wisdom, and that of all about me, seemed insufficient for the day."

Holy, righteous God, I sense that same longing to be in profound communion with You because I need vision, wisdom, and courage no one else can provide. I long for my prayers to be a consistent commitment to be on Your side rather than an appeal for You to join my causes. Forgive me when I act like I have a corner on the truth and always am right. Then my prayers reach no further than the ceiling. In humility, I spread out my concerns before You and ask for Your inspiration. You have taught me to pray, "Your will be done on earth as it is in heaven."

Dear God, I do not need to ask to come into Your presence, for You have been ever-present through my nights and days. I never need shout across the spaces to You as an absent God. You are nearer than my own soul and closer than my most secret thoughts. I need not inform You of my requests, for You are omniscient. I do not need to brief You on the alternative possibilities for today's decisions, for You already know what is in keeping with Your best for me and will reveal that if I ask You.

What I do need is to linger in Your presence until I am assured of Your love, regain true security, and am refortified by Your strength. Thank You for using this time of prayer with You to show me Your faithfulness and to give me Your guidance. Amen.

When you pray, you shall not be like the hypocrites. For they love to pray standing in the synagogues and on the corners of the streets, that they may be seen by men. Assuredly, I say to you, they have their reward. But you, when you pray, go into your room, and when you have shut your door, pray to your Father who is in the secret place; and your Father who sees in secret will reward you openly. And when you pray, do not use vain repetitions as the heathen do. For they think that they will be heard for their many words.

Therefore do not be like them. For your Father knows the things you have need of before you ask Him. In this manner, therefore, pray:

Our Father in heaven,
Hallowed be Your name.
Your kingdom come.
Your will be done
On earth as it is in heaven.
Give us this day our daily bread.
And forgive us our debts,
As we forgive our debtors.
And do not lead us into temptation,
But deliver us from the evil one.
For Yours is the kingdom and the
power and the glory forever. Amen.

For if you forgive men their trespasses, your heavenly Father will also forgive you. But if you do not forgive men their trespasses, neither will your Father forgive your trespasses.

MATTHEW 6:5-15

❧❧❧

PART VII

IN TIMES WHEN GOD HIMSELF IS THE ANSWER TO PRAYER

When I Need God Himself More than His Gifts

୧୨୦୦୨୦

JULIAN OF NORWICH in the fifteenth century prayed,

> God of Your Goodness, give me Yourself,
> for You are sufficient for me…
> If I were to ask anything less
> I should always be in want,
> for in You alone do I have all.

Loving Father, I come to You seeking the ultimate joy of life: I simply come to abide simply in Your presence. I would not interrupt what You have to say to me with chatter. I need You more than anything that You can provide for me. Make me as ready to listen as I am to talk. You have created me for communion with You. I thank You for speaking to me in my soul. Now I hear what You have been seeking to tell me: I am loved, forgiven, and cherished by You. You have plans for me and a personal will for me. I open my mind and heart to receive You—my Lord, Saviour, Peace, and Power.

Your presence is with me even when I become busy and momentarily forget You. Thank You for continually breaking through the barriers of insensitivity with the overtures of Your love. You are my closest Friend, as well as my God. Help me to keep that friendship in good working order. Lord, You know me. I get so absorbed in my activities and begin to think I am capable of functioning without Your strength. Show me the mediocrity of my efforts without Your interventions and inspiration. I dedicate this day to live for Your glory and by Your grace, sustained by Your goodness. You are my Lord and Saviour. Amen.

Abide in Me, and I in you. As the branch cannot
bear fruit of itself, unless it abides in the vine,
neither can you, unless you abide in Me.

JOHN 15:4

By this we know that we abide in Him,
and He in us, because He has given us of His Spirit.

1 JOHN 4:13

As the deer pants for the water brooks, so pants my soul for
You, O God. My soul thirsts for God, for the living God.

PSALM 42:1-2

"Let him who glories glory in this,
That he understands and knows Me,
That I am the LORD, exercising lovingkindness, judgment
and righteousness in the earth.
For in these I delight," says the LORD.

JEREMIAH 9:24

Because Your lovingkindness is better than life,
My lips shall praise You.
Thus I will bless You while I live.

PSALM 63:3-4

When My Inner Eyes
Need Focus

ᏀᎬᎧᎧᎦ

ᎯLMIGHTY GOD, IT IS WITH Your permission that I am alive, by Your grace that I have been prepared for my work, by Your appointment that I am here, and by Your blessing that I am secure in the gifts and talents that You have given me. Renew my body with health and strength. Open my inner eyes so I can see things and people with Your perspective. Teach me new truth today. May I never be content with what I have learned or think I know. Set me free to soar with wings of joy and delight. I trade in the spirit of self-importance for the spirit of self-sacrifice, the need to appear great for the desire to make others great, the worry over my place of importance for the certainty of Your place in my heart. Restore the continuous flow of Your Spirit through me as a mighty river.

Dear God, You are Jehovah-Shammah, who promises to be with me whenever and wherever I need you throughout this day. You have assured me that You will never leave or forsake me. You remind me that Your love is there when I am insecure, Your strength when I am stretched beyond my resources, Your guidance when I must make decisions, Your hope when I am tempted to be discouraged, Your patience when difficult people distress me, Your joy when I get grim.

I open my mind to receive Your divine intelligence, my responsibilities to glorify You, my relationships to express Your amazing affirmation, my face to radiate Your care and concern. As You care for me today, I pledge myself to live for Your glory. I am ready to receive what I will need each hour—each challenge, each opportunity. This day is a gift, and I accept it gratefully. You are my Lord and Saviour. Amen.

Bless the LORD, O my soul; and all that is within me, bless His holy name! Bless the LORD, O my soul, and forget not all His benefits: who forgives all your iniquities, who heals all your diseases, who redeems your life from destruction, who crowns you with lovingkindness and tender mercies, who satisfies your mouth with good things, so that your youth is renewed like the eagle's.

PSALM 103:1-5

He took the blind man by the hand and led him out of the town. And when He had spit on his eyes and put His hands on him, He asked him if he saw anything. And he looked up and said, "I see men like trees, walking." Then He put His hands on his eyes again and made him look up. And he was restored and saw everyone clearly.

MARK 8:22-25

Be Thou my Vision, O Lord of my heart;
Naught be all else to me, save that Thou art
Thou my best Thought, by day or by night,
Waking or sleeping, Thy presence my light.
Riches I heed not, nor man's empty praise,
Thou mine Inheritance, now and always:
Thou and Thou only, first in my heart,
High King of Heaven, my Treasure Thou art.

Irish, translated by Mary Byrne

Open my eyes that I may see
Glimpses of truth Thou hast for me;
Place in my hands the wonderful key
That shall unclasp and set me free.
Silently now I wait for Thee
Ready, my God, Thy will to see
Open my eyes, illumine me,
Spirit divine.

Clara H. Scott

When I Need Trifocal Lenses

This is the day the LORD has made;
We will rejoice and be glad in it.

PSALM 118:24

•••

EVER-LOVING GOD, I THANK YOU for the quiet rest of night, for the promise that has come with this new day, and for the hope I feel. While I slept, I rested under the shadow of Your love. Now as sleep has been washed from the eyes of my mind, implant them with trifocal lenses, so that I may behold Your signature in the natural world around me, see the needs of people so I can care for them with sensitivity, and visualize the work that I must do. With a mind alert and heart at full attention, I salute You as my Sovereign. Thank You for meeting all the needs of my body, soul, and spirit so I can serve You with renewed dedication. As you hover around me as I pray, grant me wisdom throughout the day.

Dear God, You give the day and show the way. You guide what I am to do and say and help me without delay. Whatever challenges I must face, You promise me Your strength and grace. You never give me more than I can take, and You guide the decisions I must make. Help me to look for vision from above and rejoice in Your unlimited love. When this day comes to an end, may I praise You for being my Father and my Friend. Amen.

I have been crucified with Christ;
it is no longer I who live, but Christ lives in me;
and the life which I now live in the flesh I live by faith
in the Son of God, who loved me and gave Himself
for me. I do not set aside the grace of God…

GALATIANS 2:20-21

To be nobody but yourself in a world which is doing
its best, night and day, to make you everybody else—
means the hardest battle which any human being can
fight, and never stop fighting.

e. e. cummings
from *The Magic Marker*

William Penn said of George Fox what I hope can be said
of all of us, "He was an original and no man's copy."

I desire so to conduct the affairs of this administra-
tion that if at the end, when I come to lay down the
reins of power, I have lost every other friend on earth,
I shall have at least one friend left, and that friend
shall be inside me.

Abraham Lincoln

Do you feel that way about the person inside you?

When I Need to See the Invisible in the Visible

❦

ALMIGHTY GOD, HELP ME TO SEE the invisible movement of Your Spirit in people and events. Beyond my everyday world of ongoing responsibilities and the march of secular history with its sinister and frightening possibilities, You call me to another world of supra-sensible reality, which is the main-spring of the universe, the environment of everyday existence, and my very life and strength at this moment. Help me to know that You are present, are working Your purposes out, and have plans for me. Give me eyes to see Your invisible pres-ence working through people, arranging details, solving com-plexities, and bringing good out of whatever difficulties I entrust to You.

I begin this new day affirming my loyalty to You, dear God. Grant me eyes to see You as the unseen but ever-present Sovereign. Then help me to claim Your promise, "Call to Me, and I will answer you, and show you great and mighty things, which you do not know" (Jeremiah 33:3). Through Christ my Lord and Saviour. Amen.

How precious also are Your thoughts to me, O God!
How great is the sum of them!

PSALM 139:17

God is not the author of confusion but of peace,
as in all the churches of the saints.

1 CORINTHIANS 14:33

To them God willed to make known what are
the riches of the glory of this mystery among the Gentiles:
which is Christ in you, the hope of glory.

COLOSSIANS 1:27

Now to the King eternal, immortal, invisible, to God
who alone is wise, be honor and glory forever and ever.
Amen.

1 TIMOTHY 1:17

I will bring the blind by a way they did not know;
I will lead them in paths they have not known.
I will make darkness light before them,
And crooked places straight.
These things I will do for them,
And not forsake them.

ISAIAH 42:16

The LORD is near to all who call upon Him,
to all who call upon Him in truth.
He will fulfill the desire of those who fear Him.

PSALM 145:18-19

When the Frantic Becomes Familiar

❦

*L*ORD, SOMETIMES I FIND BEING FRANTIC more familiar than the pleasure of being calm. I actually look for distress because it is more familiar to me than being confidently quiet. Even among believing, committed Christians, the old patterns of agitated nerves, overpressured schedules, conflicts with people, and disturbing stress have become so much the expected that I am in danger of making difficulties bigger than they are.

I hear a great deal these days about the problem of noise pollution. I live in a noisy society that keeps me in constant agitation. Added to the clashing, clanging noise of our congested, urbanized, jet-travel society, I am bombarded by the endless sounds of television, radio, and the omnipresent blaring of music systems in most every store or office in which I find myself. And then there's the distressing impact of ringing telephones, the whir of all our machines and appliances in our highly mechanized living.

But that's not all, Lord. I am a part of a culture that talks because it doesn't know what it wants to say. We abhor quiet like nature abhors a vacuum. Talk, talk, talk! We talk it over, talk it up, and talk it through. And yet, with all our talking we still fail to understand each other.

And finally, I am polluted by the "noise" of so much of what I read. It is the bad news—the jangling news that makes block-letter headlines. I am bombarded by the bold print that describes terrorist action, threat of nuclear war, murder, kidnapping, and suffering.

All this keeps me on edge and distraught. How can I take it? The point is—I can't! It is impossible to handle it unless I possess an inner calm and quietness. Without that, my external world of clamor and noise become unbearable.

You offer me a promise for the problem of inner tension: "Be still, and know that I am God; I will be exalted among the nations, I will be exalted in the earth! The LORD of hosts is with us; the God of Jacob is our refuge" (Psalm 46:10-11).

You have shown me the deeper meaning of the Hebrew for "be still." It really means "leave off." The implication is, "let up, let go, ease off." Stillness is surrender. It's being willing to do nothing until I am able to allow You to do what only You can do and You have given me clear direction of what You want me to do. I will be still, Lord, today. Even now I feel the result. My inner world is at peace, and You will give me power to change my outer world. Thank You, Lord…being frantic feels a whole lot less familiar. Amen.

With eyes wide open to the mercies of God, I beg you, my brothers, as an act of intelligent worship, to give him your bodies, as a living sacrifice, consecrated to him and acceptable by him. Don't let the world around you squeeze you into its own mold, but let God re-mold your minds from within, so that you may prove in practice that the plan of God for you is good, meets all his demands and moves towards the goal of true maturity.

ROMANS 12:1-2 PHILLIPS

When I Need to Wait on God

❦

$\mathcal{D}$EAR GOD, THINK YOUR THOUGHTS through me today. I want to love You with my mind and praise You with my intellect. I seek to be a riverbed for the mighty flow of Your wisdom through me. Teach me to wait on You, to experience deep calm of soul, and then to receive Your guidance. I spread out before You the decisions I must make. Thank You in advance for Your guidance. Give me the humility to trust You for answers and solutions, and then grant me the courage to do what time alone with You has convinced me must be done. You are the author of all truth and the bottomless sea of understanding.

Send Your Spirit into my mind and illuminate my understanding with insight and discernment. I accept the admonition of Proverbs, "Incline your ear to wisdom, and apply your heart to understanding; yes, if you cry out for discernment, and lift up your voice for understanding, if you seek her as silver, and search for her as for hidden treasures; then you will understand the fear of the LORD, and find the knowledge of God. For the LORD gives wisdom; from His mouth come knowledge and understanding" (Proverbs 2:2-6). Amen.

There are days of silent sorrow
In the seasons of our life;
There are wild despairing moments.
There are hours of mental strife;
There are times of stony anguish,
When the tears refuse to fall;
But the waiting time, my brothers,
Is the hardest time of all…

We can bear the heat of conflict,
Though the sudden, crushing blow,
Beating back our gathered forces,
For a moment lay us low;
We may rise again beneath it
None the weaker for the fall,
But the waiting time, my brothers,
Is the hardest time of all.

—*Sara Doudney*

When I Need
a Healing of Memories

❦

CHRIST, THE HEALER OF MEMORIES, thank You for clearing the memories I harbor of my failures, mistakes, and inadequacies. I know if those memories are not forgiven and cleansed, they will fester in me. Eventually they will congeal into an overall attitude of self-condemnation or dread. I need to hear and appropriate your words: "Neither do I condemn you." Then I need to say that to myself—and finally, to people who may have hurt me.

My confession is not so that I may be forgiven, but because I know I already am. In this quiet prayer time with You, I ask You to help me list out distressing things I've done or others have done to me. As the memories begin to flow and as each one is focused, I ask for your forgiveness and the power to forgive myself and others.

Thank You for Your total absolution. May I be as generous with others as You have been to me. Help me communicate in words the forgiveness I feel. Today is the day to say, "I forgive you." I will engage in reconciling conversations, phone calls, or letters. Help me not to put it off. I will not use the opportunity to remind people of how much they hurt or troubled me, but will simply assure them of Your forgiveness and love, and mine. I will follow up my words with actions of affirmation and reassurance.

Lord, help me to gather up my hurting memories and unload them to You on a consistent basis. You motivate this desire and are always ready to heal me and enable me to be a healing agent with others. Amen.

"Come now, and let us reason together,"
Says the LORD. "Though your sins are like scarlet,
They shall be as white as snow;
Though they are red like crimson,
They shall be as wool."

ISAIAH 1:18

Out of the depths I have cried to You, O LORD;
Lord, hear my voice! Let Your ears be attentive to the voice
of my supplications. If You, LORD, should mark iniquities,
O Lord, who could stand? But there is forgiveness
with You, that You may be feared.

PSALM 130:1-4

The LORD is gracious and full of compassion, slow to anger
and great in mercy. The LORD is good to all,
and His tender mercies are over all His works…
The LORD is near to all who call upon Him,
to all who call upon Him in truth.
He will fulfill the desire of those who fear Him;
He will also hear their cry and save them.

PSALM 145:8-9,18-19

The Spirit of the Lord is upon Me,
because He has anointed Me
to preach the gospel to the poor;
He has sent Me to heal the brokenhearted…

LUKE 4:18

Do you want to be made well?

JOHN 5:6

PRAYING THROUGH THE TOUGH TIMES

When I Need to Give Thanks

❧❧❧

LORD, I READ THE BIBLE and there it is: the persistently repeated admonition to give thanks. I know You well enough to know that You do not need the assurance of my gratitude. Surely, the need for thanksgiving must have something to do with my spiritual health. The psalmist said, "O LORD my God, I will give thanks to You forever" (Psalm 30:12). In this life and in heaven, forever is a long time. Paul said, "In everything give thanks; for this is the will of God for you" (1 Thessalonians 5:18).

In everything, Lord? Suddenly I know the secret. Thanksgiving is the memory of the heart. I have great memories of Your faithfulness. They become cherished memories as I tell You how grateful I am, not only for Your blessings, but, for You. I say with Joyce Kilmer, "Thank God for God!"

Most important of all, I know that when I thank You for all Your good gifts, the growth of false pride is stunted. And when I can thank You even for the rough and tough things in life, I really can let go of my control and trust You to bring good out of the most distressing things. And so, I give thanks!

I close this prayer of gratitude with special thanks for Christ—His life, message, death, resurrection, and presence. In His majesty and power I pray. Amen.

Enter into His gates with thanksgiving,
And into His courts with praise.
Be thankful to Him, and bless His name.
For the Lord is good;
His mercy is everlasting,
And His truth endures to all generations.

Psalm 100:4-5

You shall rejoice in every good thing
which the Lord Your God has given you.

Deuteronomy 26:11

It is good to give thanks to the Lord,
And to sing praises to Your name, O Most High;
To declare Your lovingkindness in the morning,
And Your faithfulness every night.

Psalm 92:1-2

Oh, give thanks to the Lord! Call upon His name;
make known His deeds among the peoples! Sing to Him,
sing psalms to Him; talk of all His wondrous works! Glory
in His holy name; let the hearts of those rejoice who seek
the Lord! Seek the Lord and His strength; seek
His face evermore! Remember His marvelous works
which He has done.

1 Chronicles 16:8-12

When I Need a Sense of the Value of Time

As for me, I trust in You, O Lord;
I say, "You are my God."
My times are in Your hand.

❧❧❧

*D*EAR GOD, A THOUSAND YEARS in Your sight are like yesterday when it is past. Lord of Time, You divide my life into years, months, weeks, and hours. As I live my life, You make me very conscious of the passage of time, the shortness of time to accomplish what I want, and my impatience with other people's priorities in the use of time. I've learned that work expands to fill the time available, but also that deadlines are a part of life.

Here I am at the beginning of a crucial day. Grant me an expeditious use of the hours of this day to accomplish what really needs to be done. Grant me an acute sense of the value of time and my accountability to You for using it wisely. I believe there is enough time in today to do what You want done. I press on without pressure, but with promptness to Your timing. You are always on time, in time, to help me in the use of time. Amen.

Just for Today

Lord, for tomorrow and its needs
    I do not pray;
Keep me, my God, from stain of sin
    Just for today.
Help me to labor earnestly
    And duly pray;
Let me be kind in word and deed,
    Father, today.

Let me no wrong or idle word
    Unthinking say;
Set Thou a seal upon my lips
    Through all today…
So for tomorrow and its needs
    I do not pray;
Still keep me, guide me, love me, Lord,
    Through each day.

Sybil F. Partridge, a.k.a. Sister Mary Xavier

When I Need
to Be Committed

❧❧❧

GRACIOUS GOD, YOU HAVE REVEALED that commitment is the key to opening the floodgates for the inflow of Your Spirit. Repeatedly, You have responded to my unreserved commitment to You when faced with challenges and problems. You have provided me with clarity of thought and ingenious solutions. Unexpected blessings happen; serendipitous events occur; people respond; and the tangled mess of details is untangled. Amazed, I look back and realize that it was the moment when I gave up, You took over; when I let go, You took hold; when I rested in You, my strength was replenished.

Today, I prayerfully personalize the assurance of the psalmist, "I commit my way to You, Lord. I also trust in You, and You will bring Your plans to pass. I rest in You, and wait patiently for You" (see Psalm 37:5,7).

Dear God, You have ordained that there is one decision I must make every day. It is the most crucial decision in the midst of all the other decisions I will be called to make. I hear Elijah's challenge, "Choose for yourselves this day whom you will serve" (Joshua 24:15).

You have given me the freedom to choose whom I will serve today. I want to renew my decision to serve You as the only Lord of my life. I know that without this decisive intentionality, I will drift into secondary loyalties. You entrust Your strength, gifts of leadership, and vision to those who start each day with a fresh decision to do everything for Your glory and according to Your specific guidance. In the quiet of this moment I make my decision to worship You and commit everything to You. You alone are my Lord and Saviour. Amen.

COMMITMENT

Commitment, because it is the final thing, is also the principal thing. A Christian is one who is committed to Jesus Christ in every way. Such commitment is the diametrical opposite of cool detachment, and for that reason it is always hazardous. Because commitment includes involvement and consequent risk, it takes courage to care. The involvement always includes actions and not mere opinions. This is why the honest repetition of a creed is really a fearsome step. The words "I believe in God" do not mean "I incline to the opinion that in all probability there exists a Being who may not inappropriately be called to God." The words, if they mean anything at all, mean the determination to live and to act in the light of declared conviction. It is to do what the Wright brothers did at Kitty Hawk. They did not merely voice the opinion that flight with a heavier-than-air machine was possible; *they got into the machine!* Insofar as we have recovered in our generation the recognition that commitment is central to the Christian life, we are supported marvelously by the final prayer of our Lord.

—⌐ *Elton Trueblood* ⌐—

When I Need Divine Inspiration

❦

$\mathcal{A}$LMIGHTY GOD, I SURRENDER MY LIFE to You, the work of this day, and the challenges I face. You have made relinquishment the condition for receiving Your grace and guidance. I accept the admonition of Proverbs: "Commit your works to the LORD, and your thoughts will be established" (Proverbs 16:3). I long to be a divinely inspired thinker. When I commit my problems, plans, and projects to You, You instigate thoughts I would not have conceived without your help. Show me how the sublime secret of intellectual inspiration works.

I claim Your presence. I praise You for Your superabundant adequacy to supply my needs spiritually and intellectually. You establish my thinking and energize my work.

Gracious God, You have promised that "in quietness and confidence shall be your strength" (Isaiah 30:15). Thank You for this prayer, in which I can commune with You, renew my convictions, receive fresh courage, and affirm my dedication to serve You. In Your presence I simply can *be*...and know that I am loved. You love me and give me new beginnings each day. Thank You that I can depend on Your guidance for all that is ahead of me this day. Suddenly I realize that this quiet moment has refreshed me. I am replenished with new hope.

Now I can return to my outer world of challenges and opportunities with greater determination. I consecrate the day; You will show the way, and I will receive Your strength without delay. You are my Lord and Saviour. Amen.

Lord, what a change within us one short hour
Spent in Thy presence will avail to make!
What heavy burdens from our bosoms take!
What parched grounds refresh as with a shower!
We kneel, and all around us seems to lower;
We rise, and all, the distant and the near,
Stands forth in sunny outline, brave and clear;
We kneel, how weak; we rise, how full of power!

Why, therefore, should we do ourselves this wrong,
Or others—that we are not always strong—
That we are sometimes overborne with care—
That we should ever weak or heartless be,
Anxious or troubled—when with us is prayer,
And joy and strength and courage are with Thee?

—◦ *Richard C. Trench* ◦—

When I Need to Be Held Accountable

❧❧❧

ALMIGHTY GOD, I PRAISE YOU for not making life a court-room without a judge. I don't have to judge myself with self-condemnation or others with harshness; You are the Judge of my life, the One to whom I must account for my behavior, character, and relationships. I expose my private and public life to Your judgment. There are no secrets from You. I spread out before You all that I have been and done, and ask You to show me what You require. I belong to You. The people of my life; Your gifts, given to me by Your divine appointment; and Your justice and righteousness are my mandates. May I see myself honestly in the pure white light of Your truth.

Sovereign God, I accept that I am accountable for the precious gift of life. You are the ultimate Judge of what I say and do. Above the opinions of people, I report to You. Sometimes I am pulled apart by trying to meet the demands and expectations of the multiplicity of factions that seek to factor my life. Help me to play my life to an audience of One: You, dear Father. You alone can give me the strength, courage, and wisdom I need. When I seek first Your pleasure, I can serve with pleasure. Take my mind and think through it; take my lips and speak through them; take my heart and set it on fire with convictions that will enable me to enable Your best for my life.

Now as I stand before You as my Judge, I feel Your Son beside me with mercy and within me as perfect peace. Take my hands, dear Lord, lead me on so that, as this day closes and I say my prayers, I may have less to confess and more for which to give thanks. In Your righteous, all-powerful name. Amen.

I said, "I will guard my ways, lest I sin with my tongue;
I will restrain my mouth with a muzzle, while
the wicked are before me." I was mute with silence, I held
my peace even from good; and my sorrow was stirred up.
My heart was hot within me; while I was musing,
the fire burned. Then I spoke with my tongue: "Lord, make
me to know my end, and what is the measure of my days,
that I may know how frail I am. Indeed, You have made
my days as handbreadths, and my age is as nothing before
You; certainly every man at his best state is but vapor.
Surely every man walks about like a shadow; surely they
busy themselves in vain; he heaps up riches, and
does not know who will gather them."

Psalm 39:1-6

Who has measured the waters in the hollow of his hand,
measured heaven with a span and calculated
the dust of the earth in a measure? Weighed the mountains
in scales and the hills in a balance? Who has directed
the Spirit of the Lord, or as His counselor has taught Him?
With whom did He take counsel, and who instructed Him,
and taught Him in the path of justice?
Who taught Him knowledge,
and showed Him the way of understanding?

Isaiah 40:12-14

May our Lord Jesus Christ Himself, and our God
and Father, who has loved us and given us everlasting consolation and good hope by grace, comfort your
hearts and establish you in every good word and work.

2 Thessalonians 2:16-17

༄༅

The most important thought I ever had was that of
my individual responsibility to God.

—༄ *Daniel Webster* ༄—

When I Need Christ's
Character Traits for My Trials

⸎⸎⸎

$\mathcal{G}$RACIOUS CHRIST, YOU HAVE TOLD ME that if I, as a branch, am connected to You, the Vine of virtue, my life will emulate Your character. I dedicate this day to live as Your branch for the flow of Your Spirit. I admit that apart from You, I can accomplish nothing of lasting significance. I ask that I may be distinguished with the fruit of Your Spirit, a cluster of divinely inspired, imputed, and induced traits of Your nature reproduced in me.

Your love encourages me and gives me security; Your joy uplifts me and gives me exuberance; Your peace floods my heart with serenity; Your patience calms my agitation over difficult people and pressured schedules; Your kindness enables me to deal with my own and other people's shortcomings; Your goodness challenges me to make a renewed commitment to absolute integrity; Your faithfulness produces trustworthiness that makes me more dependable; Your gentleness reveals the might of true meekness, that humbly draws on Your power; Your Lordship gives me self-control because I have accepted Your control of my life.

You are the mighty God. Live in me, Lord, and manifest in me what You want to express through me. You make me strong for tough times! Amen.

I am the vine, you are the branches.
He who abides in Me, and I in him, bears much fruit;
for without Me you can do nothing. If anyone does not
abide in Me, he is cast out as a branch and is withered;
and they gather them and throw them into the fire, and they
are burned. If you abide in Me, and My words abide in you,
you will ask what you desire, and it shall be done for you.
By this My Father is glorified, that you bear
much fruit; so you will be My disciples.

As the Father loved Me, I also have loved you;
abide in My love. If you keep My commandments you
will abide in My love, just as I have kept My Father's
commandments and abide in His love.

These things I have spoken to you, that My joy may
remain in you, and that your joy may be full.
This is My commandment, that you love one another as I
have loved you. Greater love has no one than this,
than to lay down one's life for his friends. You are My friends
if you do whatever I command you. No longer do I call you
servants, for a servant does not know what his master is
doing; but I have called you friends, for all things that I
heard from My Father I have made known to you.
You did not choose Me, but I chose you and appointed you
that you should go and bear fruit, and that your fruit
should remain, that whatever you ask the Father in My
name He may give you. These things I command you,
that you love one another.

John 15:5-17

The fruit of the Spirit is love, joy, peace, longsuffering,
kindness, goodness, faithfulness, gentleness, self-control.

Galatians 5:22-23

When the Idols of
My Heart Must Go

Holy, holy, holy, Lord God Almighty! Heaven and earth are filled with Your glory. Praise and thanksgiving be to You, Lord most high. Ruler of the universe, reign in me. Creator of all, recreate my heart to love You above all else. Provider of limitless blessings, may I never forget that I have been blessed to be a blessing.

I commit my life to You. I surrender the false idols of my heart: pride, position, power, past accomplishments. Without You, I could not breathe a breath, think a thought, or devise a plan. May my only source of security be that I have been called to be both Your friend and Your servant. You are the reason for living, the only One I must please, and the One to whom I am ultimately accountable. With complete trust, I dedicate the work of this day to You.

I hear Your assurance, "Be not afraid, I am with you." I place my hope in Your problem-solving power, Your conflict-resolving presence, and Your anxiety-dissolving peace.

Lord, You have helped me discover the liberating power of an unreserved commitment to You. When I commit my life to You and each of the challenges I face, I am not only released from the tension of living on my own limited resources, but I begin to experience the mysterious movement of Your providence. The company of heaven plus people and circumstances begin to rally to my aid. Unexpected resources are released; unexplainable good things start happening. I claim the promise of Psalm 37: "Commit your way to the LORD, trust also in Him, and He shall bring it to pass" (verse 5). Thank You, dear God, for doing it today! Amen.

Everyone…who sets up his idols in his heart,
and puts before him what causes him to stumble into
iniquity…I the LORD will answer him who comes,
according to the multitude of his idols, that I may
seize…their heart, because they are…estranged
from Me by their idols.

 EZEKIEL 14:4-5

Pride grows in the human heart like lard on a pig.

— Alexander Solzhenitsyn —

Nothing will or can restore order until our hearts
make one decision: God shall be exalted above all else.

— A. W. Tozer —

The dearest idol I have known
Whate'er that idol be
Help me to tear it from Thy throne
And worship only Thee.

— William Cowper —

The moment one definitely commits oneself, then
providence moves too. All sorts of things occur to help
one that would never otherwise have occurred. A
whole stream of events issues from the decision, raising
in one's favor all manner of unforeseen incidents and
meetings and material assistance which no man could
have dreamed would have come his way. Whatever you
can do, or dream you can, begin it. Boldness has
genius, power and magic in it. Begin it now.

— Johann Wolfgang von Goethe —

PRAYING THROUGH THE TOUGH TIMES

When Absolute Honesty
Is Required

❧❧❧

LORD GOD OF TRUTH, who calls me to absolute honesty in everything I say, I renew my commitment to truth. In a time in which people no longer expect to hear the truth, or what's worse, don't see the need consistently to speak it, make me a straight arrow who hits the target of absolute honesty. Help me to be a person on whom others always can depend for unswerving integrity.

Thank You for keeping me from those little white lies that later need big black ones to cover them up. May the reliability of my words earn me the right to give righteous leadership. Thank you for the wonderful freedom that comes from a consistency between what I promise and what I do. You are present where truth is spoken.

Spirit of the living God, fall afresh on me. I need Your strength. The wells of my own resources run dry. I need Your strength to fill up my diminished reserves—silent strength that flows into me with artesian resourcefulness, quietly filling me with renewed power. You alone can provide strength to think clearly, to decide decisively, and to speak honestly. Amen.

Put off…the old man…and be renewed in the spirit of your
mind, and…put on the new man which was created
according to God, in righteousness and true holiness.

Therefore, putting away lying, "Let each one of you speak
truth with his neighbor," for we are members of one
another. "Be angry, and do not sin": do not let the sun go
down on your wrath, nor give place to the devil. Let him
who stole steal no longer, but rather let him labor, working
with his hands what is good, that he may have something to
give him who has need. Let no corrupt word proceed out of
your mouth, but what is good for necessary edification, that
it may impart grace to the hearers. And do not grieve the
Holy Spirit of God, by whom you were sealed for the day of
redemption. Let all bitterness, wrath, anger, clamor, and evil
speaking be put away from you, with all malice. And be
kind to one another, tenderhearted, forgiving one another,
even as God in Christ forgave you.

Ephesians 4:22-32

❧❧❧

When God Himself
Is the Answer

⊱≷⊰⊱≷⊰

DEAR GOD, YOU, YOURSELF, ARE THE ANSWER to my prayers. So often I come to You with my long list of requests. Prayer becomes a "gimme" game rather than a grace gift. Help me to realize that whatever You give or withhold from me in prayer is to draw me into deeper intimacy with You. When I put the primary emphasis on a relationship with You, experiencing Your presence and receiving Your power, life becomes a privilege and loses its strain and stress. Added to that, You provide the spiritual gifts I need of wisdom and discernment, emotional strength and stability, and physical stamina and endurance. Grant me a special measure of Your inspiration today as I listen to You. Speak to me before I speak to the people in my life.

In the quiet of this magnificent moment of conversation with You, I dedicate this day. I want to live it to Your glory, alert to the dangers of this time, but without anxiety, prepared but not perplexed. I praise You that it is Your desire to give Your presence and blessings to those who ask You. You give strength and power to Your people when we seek You above anything else. You guide the humble and teach them Your way. Help me to humble myself as I live this day so that no self-serving agenda or self-aggrandizing attitude will block Your blessings. I say with the psalmist, "God be merciful to us and bless us, and cause His face to shine upon us, that Your way may be known on earth, Your salvation among all nations" (Psalm 67:1-2). You are my Lord and Saviour. Amen.

It's amazing how few Christians today have claimed the power of the indwelling Lord. They believe in Him as Saviour but sidestep His lordship over their inner hearts. W.E. Sangster put it pointedly:

> It is not enough—let it be said reverently—it is not enough to have Christ near to us. Oh, it is wonderful, of course, in contrast with not even believing in His existence at all or knowing Him only as a name, but, for the highest spiritual life, it is not enough. You see, we do most of our living inside us. Our thinking, feeling, and willing are all within. External events press upon us, but they have meaning only by our inward interpretation. We discover that when we are dealing with the troubles of life. The important thing is not what happens to us but what happens in us. The same thing can happen to two different people and a precisely different thing happens in them...
>
> If, therefore, we are to be helped in our battle against temptation and in our war with fear and worry, selfishness, and greed, we must have help within. Not there, but here! Not outside, but inside.

When I Need the Wells of My Soul Refilled with Joy

Make a joyful noise to the LORD, all you lands!
Serve the LORD with gladness;
Come before His presence with singing.
Know that the LORD, He is God.

PSALM 100:1-3

JOYOUS CHRIST, I PRAISE YOU for Your joy that is an outward expression of Your grace. When I experience Your giving, forgiving, unqualified love, the ecstasy of the joy of heaven fills my heart with an exuberant joy. Your joy is so much greater than happiness—which is dependent on circumstances, the attitudes of others, and being free from problems. Thank You that Your joy flows within me with artesian force regardless of what is occurring to me or around me. Fill the wells of my soul with Your joy that nothing can dry up, so that I can express joy regardless of what happens. You are by my side, You are on my side, and You are abiding inside to make me a communicator of affirmation and encouragement to others. Your joy fails not; it's fresh each new day—new zest for each challenge and courage for each step of the way. Thank You for Your lasting joy! Amen.

Lasting Joy

Delight yourself…in the LORD,
And He shall give you the desires of your heart.
Commit your way to the LORD,
Trust also in Him,
And He shall bring it to pass.
He shall bring forth your righteousness as the light,
And your justice as the noonday.
Rest in the LORD, and wait patiently for Him.

PSALMS 37:4-7

You shall go out with joy, and be led out with peace; the mountains and the hills shall break forth into singing before you, and all the trees of the field shall clap their hands.

ISAIAH 55:12

Peace does not mean the end of all our striving,
Joy does not mean the drying of our tears;
Peace is the power that comes to souls arriving
Up to the light where God Himself appears.
Joy is the wine that God is ever pouring
Into the hearts of those who strive with Him,
Light'ning their eyes to vision and adoring,
Strength'ning their arms to warfare glad and grim.

—*G.A. Studdert Kennedy*—
from the poem "The Suffering God"

When I Long for Friendship with Christ

❧❧❧

GRACIOUS LORD JESUS, I NEED TO KNOW You as my friend. It is not for some specific blessing I ask, but for the greatest of all blessings, the one from which all others flow. I dare to ask You for a renewal of the wonderful friendship that makes the conversation called prayer a natural give-and-take divine dialogue. In this sacred moment, I open myself to receive this gift of divine companionship with You. Why is it that I am amazed that You know me better than I know myself? Show me what I need to ask of You so You can demonstrate Your generosity once again.

Open my mind so I may see myself and my relationships from Your perspective. Reveal to me Your priorities, Your plan. I spread out before You my problems and perplexities. Help me to listen attentively to the answers You will give. I ask You to be my unseen, but undeniable, friend.

I hear Your voice sounding in my soul—"Take courage, it is I, the Lord; I am with you!" You have shown me repeatedly that courage is mine because You have taken hold of me. I can take the challenges of life because You have a tight grip on me. I say again with Horatius Bonar, "Let me no more my comfort draw from my frail hold on Thee. Rather in this rejoice with awe—Thy mighty grasp on me!"

So often I am driven to my knees to seek Your will. Then You lead me to attempt what I could not pull off in my own strength. I discover that courage is Your gift for answered prayer. At the very moment I cry out for help, You open the floodgates of courage and give me that inner resolve that makes me bold and resolute. Thank you, dear Jesus, my friend, for the fresh supply of courage to be unafraid today.

May my communion with You go deeper as the day unfolds. This is the day You have made; I will "rejoice and be glad in it" (Psalm 118:24). Amen.

I want you to meet my best friend. I've known Him for 56 years. He's been with me through trials and tragedies, pain and persecution, ups and downs, success and failure. He is the kind of friend who knows all about me and never goes away. He has a special way of helping me to see myself and do something about it. He accepts me the way I am, and yet that very acceptance makes me want to be all that I was meant to be in spite of all the difficulties around me.

He laughs with me over my mistakes and weeps with me in my sorrows. He has been faithful all through life's battles. I have never been left alone when I suffered criticism, hostility, or resistance for doing what love demanded. He is with me when truth triumphs and is always there to absorb the anguish of defeat in a righteous cause. We share a vision, a hope, a dream together…my friend and I. As a matter of fact, He gives me the daring to be true to what I believe regardless of cost.

He meets all the qualifications of a real friend: He loves without limit; He is loyal when others turn away; He listens to my hurts; and He liberates me to grasp life with gusto, regardless of the consequences. I have only one hope: when I come to the end of this portion of heaven and pass on to the next, the one thing people will remember is that I was His friend. My best friend is Jesus Christ!

❧

No longer do I call you servants, for a servant
does not know what his master is doing; but I have called
you friends, for all things that I have heard from My Father
I have made known to you. You did not choose Me,
but I chose you and appointed you that you should go and
bear fruit, and that your fruit should remain, that whatever
you ask the Father in My name He may give you.

JOHN 15:15-16

Steps to Peace with God

1. RECOGNIZE GOD'S PLAN—PEACE AND LIFE

   The message in this book stresses that God loves you and wants you to experience His peace and life.

   The BIBLE says . . . For God loved the world so much that He gave His only Son, so that everyone who believes in Him may not die but have eternal life. John 3:16

2. REALIZE OUR PROBLEM—SEPARATION

   People choose to disobey God and go their own way. This results in separation from God.

   The BIBLE says . . . Everyone has sinned and is far away from God's saving presence. Romans 3:23

3. RESPOND TO GOD'S REMEDY—CROSS OF CHRIST

   God sent His Son to bridge the gap. Christ did this by paying the penalty of our sins when He died on the cross and rose from the grave.

   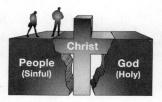

   The BIBLE says . . . But God has shown us how much He loves us—it was while we were still sinners that Christ died for us! Romans 5:8

4. RECEIVE GOD'S SON—LORD AND SAVIOR

   You cross the bridge into God's family when you ask Christ to come into your life.

   The BIBLE says . . . Some, however, did receive Him and believed in Him; so He gave them the right to become God's children. John 1:12

THE INVITATION IS TO:

REPENT (turn from your sins) and by faith RECEIVE Jesus Christ into your heart and life and follow Him in obedience as your Lord and Savior.

PRAYER OF COMMITMENT

"Lord Jesus, I know I am a sinner. I believe You died for my sins. Right now, I turn from my sins and open the door of my heart and life. I receive You as my personal Lord and Savior. Thank You for saving me now. Amen."

If you are committing your life to Christ, please let us know!
Billy Graham Evangelistic Association
1 Billy Graham Parkway, Charlotte, NC 28201-0001
1-877-2GRAHAM (1-877-247-2426)
www.billygraham.org